D1489977

CHRISTMAS CROSS STITCH

OVER 500 FESTIVE MOTIFS AND DESIGNS

CLAIRE CROMPTON

David and Charles

A DAVID & CHARLES BOOK

Copyright © David & Charles Limited 2007

David & Charles is an F+W Publications Inc. company
4700 East Galbraith Road
Cincinnati, OH 45236

First published in the UK in 2007

Text and designs copyright © Claire Crompton 2007

Photography copyright © David & Charles 2007

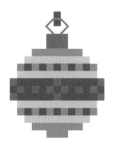

Claire Crompton has asserted her right to be identified as author of this work
in accordance with the Copyright, Designs and Patents Act, 1988.

All rights reserved. No part of this publication may be reproduced, stored in a
retrieval system, or transmitted, in any form or by any means, electronic or
mechanical, by photocopying, recording or otherwise, without prior
permission in writing from the publisher.

The designs in this book are copyright and must not be stitched for resale.

The author and publisher have made every effort to ensure that all the
instructions in the book are accurate and safe, and therefore cannot accept
liability for any resulting injury, damage or loss to persons or property,
however it may arise.

Names of manufacturers, fabric ranges and other products are provided
for the information of readers, with no intention to infringe copyright
or trademarks.

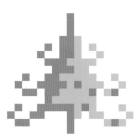

A catalogue record for this book is available from the British Library.

ISBN-13: 978-0-7153-2475-2 hardback
ISBN-10: 0-7153-2475-6 hardback

ISBN-13: 978-0-7153-2860-6 paperback
ISBN-10: 0-7153-2860-3 paperback

Printed in China by RR Donnelley

for David & Charles

Brunel House, Newton Abbot, Devon

Executive Editor Cheryl Brown
Desk Editor Bethany Dymond
Project Editor and Chart Preparation Lin Clements
Senior Designer Charly Bailey
Production Controller Ros Napper
Photography Kim Sayer and Michael Crocker

Visit our website at www.davidandcharles.co.uk

David & Charles books are available from all good bookshops; alternatively
you can contact our Orderline on 0870 9908222 or write to us at FREEPOST
EX2 110, D&C Direct, Newton Abbot, TQ12 4ZZ (no stamp required UK only);
US customers call 800-289-0963 and Canadian customers call 800-840-5220.

Contents

Introduction

For many of us the weeks before Christmas are probably the most exciting of the year and the perfect excuse to stitch, stitch, stitch! This book has been specially created to provide you with a multitude of fabulous Christmas motifs perfect for crafting unique cross stitch items.

In this book, you will find a truly wonderful collection of designs in a wide range of different styles: whether your taste is for country-style, romantic Victorian, opulent traditional, bright contemporary or full of quirky fun, you will find motifs here to delight you.

The projects shown throughout the first section give you a taste of how the motifs can be used – to craft beautiful cards, decorate gorgeous gifts, create lovely keepsakes or bring the house alive with Christmas cheer. There are also plenty of alphabets, sayings, verses and greetings, both traditional and humorous, so you can personalize your designs.

The book also contains a wealth of ideas, including using embroidery threads and beads to add texture and sparkle to your stitching; making and embellishing greetings cards; using the designs as patches or on bands to decorate gifts, garlands and garments, and designing your own Christmas sampler. Framing and making up instructions for the projects shown are included.

Using the many motifs in this book will not only give you hours of pleasurable, relaxing stitching but let you celebrate the festive season in memorable style. Whether you choose to give the embroideries away as gifts or keep them to decorate your house at Christmas time, the fabulous range of designs will fire your imagination, for Christmas now and for many years to come.

☆ *Stitch for Christmas* ☆

Country Christmas Decorations

The charming folk-art projects shown opposite are full of peaceful charm and are perfect for creating your own unique country-style Christmas. The charts are on pages 42/43.

Stitch counts

Heart Garland 36h x 37w (each heart); Peace, Joy and Love Angels 43h x 28w (each angel)

Finished design sizes

Heart Garland (each heart) 6.5 x 6.5cm (2½ x 2½in); Angels (each) 7.8 x 5cm (3 x 2in)

Stitch the designs over one block of 14-count cream Aida using two strands of stranded cotton (floss) for cross stitch and French knots and one strand for backstitch.

Heart Garland: Stitch a heart in each colourway (using the alternate thread codes on the chart), leaving 5cm (2in) between each heart. Use the alphabet on page 98 to write your own message. See page 23 for creating the hearts and making up the garland.

Angels: Stitch an angel in each colourway. The designs are made up in three ways – as a card, a gift bag and a decoration – see page 23 for making up.

Materials and Threads

It is impossible to resist some of the fabulous fabrics and threads now available – especially at Christmas time, when there are many colours specially designed for festive stitching. Because most of the designs in this book are small and quick to stitch, they will give you the perfect excuse to experiment with different fabrics and threads.

Fabrics don't have to be just white and cream: try red or green and see the simplest design come to life. Black may seem a strange choice at Christmas but what a glorious atmosphere it creates in the Nativity Sampler on page 19. At this time of year fabrics shot through with gold or silver are so much more interesting than plain equivalents. Many of the charts use white to depict snow so stitch them on icy blue for a wintry feel, or on deep blue for a night sky to highlight stars or snowflakes (see the sampler idea on page 18).

Use the background fabric to echo the chart theme – the Advent Calendar (page 17) is stitched on a sage green to follow the Shaker theme. Antique rose or grey blue could also have been used as these colours appear in the chart. Gather thread colours together to get an overall idea of the colour theme. More contemporary designs, such as the stocking and mitten garlands on page 25, would look better stitched on a crisp green or mustard gold, while the Victorian designs (pages 64/65) require more opulent colours. Make sure that colours used around the outside of the design aren't too close to the background colour or they will 'disappear'.

Threads, threads and more threads – the variety now is simply irresistible. Stranded cottons in every colour under the sun, smooth silks, glittering metallics, gleaming blending filaments, beautifully coloured variegated threads – all are hard to resist, so don't try! The designs in this book use DMC stranded cotton and some also use DMC Light Effects, a range of metallic threads ideal for bringing a festive glitter to a variety of projects, such as the Christmas carol designs on pages 26/27 and the Christmas trees on pages 58/59.

Seek out other thread ranges that may include thicker metallic threads to be used on their own; compare them with the shade in the chart key to get a good colour match. There are also space-dyed variegated threads in festive shades that can be used to stitch a border of a line of stitches; the colour will change stitch by stitch to add extra colour to a design.

☆ Stitch for Christmas ☆

Tree Decorations

These sparkly tree decorations show what can be achieved with imaginative use of fabrics and threads. You could also use the designs for small cards or gift tags. See pages 50/51 for the charts and page 23 for making up the decorations.

Stitch counts

Peace on Earth 30h x 30w;
Star Bauble 29h x 29w;
Stocking 35h x 29w;
Bethlehem Bauble 38h x 16w

Finished design sizes

Peace on Earth 5.5cm (2⅛in) square;
Star Bauble 5cm (2in) diameter;
Stocking 6.5 x 5.5cm (2½ x 2in);
Bethlehem Bauble 7 x 3cm (2¾ x 1⅛in)

Stitch the decorations over two threads of 28-count pale blue evenweave or one block of 14-count cream Aida, using two strands of stranded cotton (floss) for cross stitch and one for backstitch. Work any tweeded cross stitches using one strand of cotton together with one strand of metallic thread. Stitch on beads using two strands (see page 21). Add tassels as appropriate, either a ready-made tassel or make your own (see page 23).

Beads and Embellishments

Stitching for Christmas is a great excuse to browse around a craft shop or online seeking out just a few of the fabulous beads and embellishments now available. The choice is tantalising – diamantes, beads by the million, rub-on and stick-on motifs and letters, self-adhesive ribbons, charms in every shape and size, jewels, flowers, filigree stars, pearl strings – the list is endless. Amid all the glitter and glamour of Christmas anything goes!

Beads are wonderful for adding sparkle, opulence and texture to embroidery. To replace the French knots in a design with beads, simply match the bead colour to the stranded cotton. Mill Hill beads are listed in the chart keys but you could use any small seed bead. Faceted beads catch the light beautifully on tree decorations. Small crystal beads could replace some stitches in a design where there is snow; for example, in the winter landscapes on pages 52/53.

Buttons and charms add an interesting three-dimensional look to embroidery or can be the focal point. The Santa Stop Here hanging (opposite) is enhanced by colourful, festive-shaped embellishments. Choose a style to match your embroidery or echo a theme. Instead of stitching snowflakes or stars use buttons instead. Or add present-shaped buttons under one of the Christmas tree charts.

Scrapbooking supplies are a great source of materials, including wood, fabric, plastic, paper and card. Paper roses, leaves, holly, ivy and mistletoe would add interesting textures to a stitched Christmas wreath. Try adding ready-made bows to a stitched present or on one of the Christmas fairies (pages 74/75). If you don't want to stitch a message, use a printed greeting.

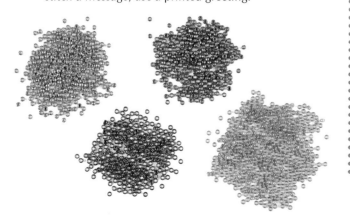

☆ Stitch for Christmas ☆

Celebration Wall Hangings

The charming wall hangings and banners shown opposite have been embellished with beads and other decorations, which turn them into something a little bit special. See pages 27, 52, 77, 89 and 97 for charts and page 16 for making up a wall hanging.

Stitch counts

Santa Stop Here 62h x 63w;
Snowy Welcome 95h x 21w;
We Three Kings 55h x 55w;
Angel 91h x 69w

Finished design sizes

Santa Stop Here 11.5 x 11.5cm (4½ x 4½in) on 14-count antique white Aida;
Snowy Welcome 15 x 3.5cm (6 x 1⅜in) on 16-count navy Aida band with gold edge;
We Three Kings 10cm (4in) square on 14-count gold Lurex Aida;
Angel 14.5 x 11cm (5¾ x 4½in) on 32-count soft blue evenweave

Stitch the motifs over two threads of evenweave or one block of Aida, using two strands of stranded cotton (floss) for cross stitch and one for backstitch. Stitch on beads using two strands (see page 21).

Santa Stop Here: secure embellishments with matching thread. Use a fun Christmas print for a backing.

Snowy Welcome Banner: use the snowflake alphabet on page 97 and snowflake buttons. Make the bottom into a point by folding the lower edge in half with right sides together and sew the two edges. Turn through to the right side. Fold the top of the banner over a mini quilt hanger, turn in the raw edge and sew down.

We Three Kings: beads highlight the richness of the Magi's clothes. Mount on a gold mini hanger and back with a rich fabric suiting the opulent theme.

Angel: embellish with a halo of five small gold stars. Use the same fabric to back the design and hang it on a dark wood bell-pull rod using gold ribbon.

Attaching Embellishments

Many embellishments are self-adhesive but others can be attached by various means, including double-sided tape, craft glue or micro glue dots. Paper or card embellishments can be stitched through with a sharp needle. Some products don't have holes to sew through so sew a few stitches across a point or around a thinner part of the shape to attach it to your embroidery. See page 21 for attaching beads.

Greetings Cards

Sending a handmade greetings card is a great way to make someone feel extra special at Christmas; especially if you personalize it. There is a wide range of aperture cards available: the apertures may be square, rectangular, circular, oval and novelty shapes – perfect for festive occasions.

Single-fold cards are easy to embellish with gorgeous ribbons, bows, charms and buttons (see page 8 for embellishment ideas). Even the smallest cross stitch embroidery can be turned into a stylish card with the addition of a bow of sheer gauze ribbon or some fine gold braid along the spine.

There are plenty of small designs in the book that are perfect for cards and could be finished in an evening, such as the gift tags (pages 72/73) or the advent calendar motifs (pages 28/29). Begin larger designs earlier to catch the last post!

Not only can you use card mounts for greetings cards but they are a quick way to frame a larger design. Add a ribbon loop at the centre top and hang with your other cards or make a sign using the alphabets (pages 96–103) or sentiments (pages 88–95) and hang from a door or in a window.

To avoid stitching a message, use printed greetings available from card-making ranges to stick on to the card.

☆ Stitch for Christmas ☆

Festive Cards

A card hanger (opposite) is perfect for displaying festive greetings cards. See pages 24, 44/45, 51 and 66 for the charts.

Stitch counts

Card Hanger 19h x 135w;
Bells 34h x 33w;
Reindeer 27h x 27w;
Candy Cane 21h x 15w;
Santa's List 50h x 39w

Finished design sizes

Card Hanger 3.5 x 24.5cm (1⅜ x 9¾in) on 14-count gold-fleck Aida;
Bells 6.2cm (2½in) square on 14-count gold-fleck Aida;
Reindeer 5cm (2in) square on 28-count light blue evenweave;
Candy Cane 5 x 3.5cm (2 x 1⅜in) on 11-count Christmas green Hardanger;
Santa's List 9 x 7cm (3½ x 2¾in) on 14-count cream Aida

Stitch the motifs over two threads of evenweave or one Aida block, using two strands of stranded cotton (floss) for cross stitch and one for backstitch (except the hanger, which uses two strands for backstitch). When working on Hardanger fabric, work over two sets of threads and use three strands for cross stitch and two for backstitch.

Card Hanger: add your own message using the alphabet on page 102 to build up the words. The finished hanger measures 6.5 x 28cm (2½ x 11in) – see page 22 for making up instructions.

Bells, Reindeer and Santa's List: mount each of the designs into double-fold aperture cards (see instructions below).

Candy Cane: trim the design to within 2cm (¾in) and fray the edges, then use double-sided tape to stick it to a single-fold card.

Using a Double-Fold Card

A double-fold card is perhaps the neatest way to present your stitched motifs. It has three sections and the stitched piece is mounted behind the middle one, which contains the aperture (see right). Before you begin, check that the design you plan to stitch will fit into the aperture. Mount the stitching into the aperture using double-sided tape or craft glue (many cards already have tape in place).

Using a Single-Fold Card

A single-fold card is simply a piece of card folded in two, with the embroidery stuck to the front of the card. Finish the design as you would when making a patch (see page 12); either turn the edges back to the wrong side and stitch down or stitch on to a backing fabric such as felt or Christmas fabric. You could also fray the edges by removing the outer row of Aida or a few threads of evenweave. Use plenty of double-sided adhesive tape to attach the embroidery to the centre of the card front.

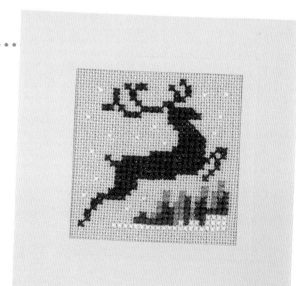

Bands and Patches

Open up a world of stitching ideas and adorn almost any item with cross stitch by working the design on Aida (or evenweave) band. Some great ideas are shown opposite, showing that you don't have to reserve your embroidery just for cards, frames or ready-made items.

Bands

Aida and evenweave bands are available in many widths, counts and colours, with different edgings and those with a gold or silver edge are well suited to festive motifs. Any small motif can be transformed into a band simply by repeating the motif along the band length – see opposite and the charts on pages 86/87 for some ideas. To make sure your design will fit on the band, see Calculating Design Size on page 20.

For the festive table, stitch the band around the edge of a tablecloth and create napkins in the same way. For napkin rings, stitch a motif on to a band and join the ends into a ring.

Bands can be applied to other items too, such as a child's scarf, with fun motifs like the penguins (page 60) or the bears (page 81), adding the child's name.

Patches

Patches are easy to make and you can stick the embroidery on paper or card using double-sided tape or craft glue. Create a special touch by sewing a patch to another piece of fabric or fuse the patch in place using double-sided interfacing (see right).

Use patches to embellish gift bags and boxes of sweets or cookies. Add them to an album of Christmas photos or use them on winter clothing.

☆ Stitch for Christmas ☆

Christmas Table Collection

Stitched bands are very versatile. The designs shown opposite are worked on 2.5cm (1in) wide and 5cm (2in) wide white 16-count Aida bands, some with a gold edging. You could use 32-count linen band.

Stitch counts

Cake Band 11h;
Jar Band 8h x 68w;
Napkin Ring 11h x 64w;
Place Mat 11h x 112w

Finished design sizes

Cake Band 2cm (¾in) high;
Jar Band 1.25 x 11cm (½ x 4¼in);
Napkin Ring 2 x 10cm (¾ x 4in);
Place Mat 2 x 18cm (¾ x 7in)

Stitch the motifs over one block of Aida (or two threads of linen), using two strands of stranded cotton (floss) for cross stitch and two for backstitch. Instructions for repeating motifs and turning corners are given with the charts on page 86. Wash embroidery before direct contact with food.

Cake Band: begin in the centre of the band and work outwards, repeating the design as often as necessary.

Jar Band: use the alphabet on page 99 for the lettering and work a holly motif on either side (mirroring the design – see motif on page 87). Change the ribbon colour to match your table linen.

Napkin Ring: Use the same alphabet as the jar band to stitch an initial and add a holly/ribbon motif either side. Cut the band to size, allowing 1.5cm (⅝in) at each end for seams and with the initial central. With right sides together join the seams.

Place Mat: work the message (or guest's name), framing it with one repeat of the motif on each side. Attach the band to a ready-made mat (see below).

Using Iron-on Interfacing

Back cross stitch embroidery with iron-on interfacing to prevent fraying when cutting the fabric into shape. Use double-sided interfacing to fuse embroidery to another fabric.

Cut a piece of interfacing a little larger than the finished design size (including any unworked fabric needed to fill an aperture or ready-made item). Set the iron to the manufacturer's recommended heating. Test on waste fabric and interfacing to make sure that they will bond without scorching the design. Place the stitching face down on a towel and iron on the interfacing, trimming off excess.

Attaching Embroidery

You can attach your embroidery to a variety of surfaces. Back it with iron-on interfacing (see above) and trim to size allowing 1.5cm (⅝in) for turnings. Turn in the edges and tack (baste). If sticking on to paper or card, stitch around the edges through all thicknesses using a stranded cotton colour used in the design. Stick double-sided adhesive tape to the back, remove the backing strip and stick into position.

If sewing the design to fabric as a patch, hem the edges if necessary, and place the design right side up on the backing fabric and sew around the edges through all thicknesses.

Ready-Made Items

There is a whole range of ready-made items that you can stitch directly on to – ideal for gifts at Christmas when time is short. There are dozens of designs in the book that are perfect for display in all sorts of ways – as little pictures, coasters, trinket pots, fridge magnets, door plates and much more. Some sweet gifts for a baby's first Christmas are shown opposite.

Look out for small frames in the shape of a Christmas tree, star or heart to hang on your tree or give as unusual Christmas cards. Stitch with metallic threads and beads to create extra sparkle.

Choose some of the lovely ceramic, glass and metal bowls with lids to accommodate your embroidery. They make beautiful gifts filled with sweets, homemade cookies or seasonal pot-pourri – use the gift tag ideas on pages 72/73 or the alphabets to put on your own message.

Younger children will love embroidered dolls or bears, as well as pencil cases and small bags to keep Christmas mementoes in. Check that the items and any embellishments used are safe for the age of the baby or child. For older children, key rings, pen holders, rulers and notebooks make fun gifts to be used during the holiday season.

Create your own festive table setting by mounting embroideries into ready-made napkin rings and coasters. Use fun designs for the children and personalize the others so everyone can have their own special napkin and coaster.

Mini bags made from Aida can be embroidered for a special gift. Stitch one with the name of each family member using the alphabets on pages 96–103, put a gift, a party hat and party popper into each one and place on the Christmas table instead of crackers.

Use fridge magnets and door plates to display seasonal messages, such as 'Santa Stop Here'.

If the design you would like to stitch won't fit into your chosen item, alter the fabric count to make it smaller or stitch a small part of the motif, omitting the background or surrounding border.

☆ Stitch for Christmas ☆

Baby's First Christmas

The baby-themed ready-made items shown opposite make a sweet collection of gifts. The charts are on pages 28/29 and 62/63.

Stitch counts

Baby's Bib 29h x 49w;
Baby's Shoes 17h x 15w (each motif);
Baby's Hat 29h x 24w;
Little Teddy 26h x 31w

Finished design sizes

Baby's Bib 5 x 9cm (2 x 3½in) on 14-count;
Baby's Shoes 3 x 2.7cm (1¼ x 1in) on 14-count;
Baby's Hat 5.3 x 4.5cm (2 x 1¾in) on 14-count;
Little Teddy 3.5 x 4.5cm (1½ x 1¾in) on 18-count

Stitch the motifs over one block of white or antique white Aida, using two strands of stranded cotton (floss) for cross stitch and one for backstitch.

Baby's Bib and Shoes: stitch the lettering along one line for the bib. Centre the motifs on the shoes by counting the number of Aida squares across the width.

Baby's Hat: if you can't find an appropriate ready-made item with an Aida panel, add a patch to a bought item. The motif on page 63 could be for a girl or boy – change the colour of the clothes to match the hat. Use the alphabet on page 99 to add your own message. See page 12 for attaching the patch.

Teddy: use the alphabet on the bottom of page 99 to create your message.

Mounting Work in Ready-Made Items

Items made to house embroidery come in all shapes and sizes so check the size of your planned stitching to ensure it will fit the item (see Calculating Design Size on page 20). It helps to back the stitched design with iron-on interfacing to stiffen it and prevent fraying (see page 12). Use paper or thin card to hide the back of any stitching.

Ready-made items are surprisingly versatile. The brass-lidded bowl shown here is stitched on 14-count white Aida but the motif could be made smaller by working on 16-count. Add a small initial in the centre and fill the bowl with chocolates as a special gift for a friend.

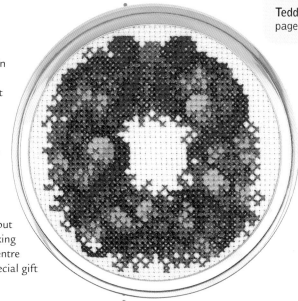

Framing and Hanging

How you frame or hang your cross stitch makes a great deal of difference to the look of the finished piece so it is worth taking a little trouble. There are some stunning frames and mounts available, both ready-made or from a professional framer. Those with gold or silver colour schemes are particularly apt for Christmas time (see The Nativity Sampler overleaf). Some designs look fine without a frame, made up as a wall hanging instead.

Display a festive collection of pictures on a wall by buying a variety of different sized frames but with the same finish and frame. The teddies on pages 78/79 would be lovely for a child's room.

Stand a framed design on your mantelpiece or on a table amongst other Christmas decorations – try one of the Christmas carol designs on pages 26/27.

Try hanging a framed picture 'on point' for a different look. The Christmas flowers wreath on page 68 would look very pretty displayed in such a way.

Wall hangings are lighter and more flexible than framed embroidery

so you can hang them on the tree, on a door, or in a window, especially if you use a small quilt hanger; these are made from wire and sometimes have a motif on them, like the heart ones on page 9. Larger designs make delightful wall hangings, as you can see by the Advent Calendar opposite. You can use wooden dowelling and bell pull ends painted to match your stitching. Choose a Christmas print or something to match your colour scheme to back the hanging.

For a quick bell pull hanging, stitch your design on to a wide Aida or evenweave band, turn under the raw edges and hang with ribbons.

☆ Stitch for Christmas ☆

Advent Calendar

This attractive advent calendar, which can be stitched as a keepsake and used every year, features the country-style motifs charted on pages 38/39 but you could also use the alternate advent motifs on pages 28/29. Wrapped sweets, tree chocolates or small gifts can be tied on to the rings using thin ribbon.

Stitch count 185h x 144w

Finished design size 33.5 x 26cm (13¼ x 10¼in)

Work over one block of 14-count sage green Aida (or over two threads of 28-count evenweave), using two strands for cross stitch and French knots and one strand for backstitch. See page 22 for full instructions on stitching and making up.

Framing a Picture

You will need: a frame to fit embroidery, mount board, thin wadding (batting), pins and double-sided adhesive tape.

1 Cut a piece of mount board to fit the frame aperture. Using double-sided tape, stick wadding to the mount board and trim to the same size.

2 Lay the embroidery right side up on to the wadding, matching a fabric thread along the edges. Push pins through at the four corners and along the edges to mark the position. Trim the fabric to leave 5cm (2in) all around.

3 Turn the embroidery and mount board over together. Stick double-sided tape around the edges of the board to a depth of 5cm (2in) and peel off the backing. Fold the excess fabric back, pressing down firmly to stick the fabric to the board, adding more tape to neaten corners. Remove pins and reassemble the frame with the embroidery in it. Omit the glass as this can flatten the stitches.

Making a Wall Hanging

You will need: backing fabric, ribbon for hanging and a small quilt hanger or wooden bell pull ends.

1 Trim the finished embroidery to leave 2.5cm (1in) all around. Cut backing fabric the same size. With right sides facing and a 1.5cm (⅝in) seam allowance, sew the two pieces together leaving the bottom seam open. Turn through to the right side and press. Sew the bottom seam closed.

2 Cut the ribbon into two lengths and fold each in half over the hanger. Pin to the wrong side of the top edge of the embroidery 2cm (¾in) from each side edge and sew neatly in place.

Designing a Christmas Sampler

The charts in this book have been presented in themes that are ideal for creating a beautiful keepsake Christmas sampler, which can be brought out each year to mark the beginning of the festivities.

Designing Your Own Sample

The nativity sampler design and the variations on this simple plan (see below) together with the suggestions here will give you ideas on how to vary the plan to create your own unique sampler using the motifs in the book.

 Choose a theme for your sampler to make it easier to select motifs.

 Vary the size of the panels to suit the motifs chosen but keep a balanced look – see Using a Sampler Plan, below.

Repeat a small motif to make a row, changing the colours of each motif.

Take part of a larger motif to make a smaller design. For example, the shops in the snow-covered village on page

52 could be worked separately and used as spot motifs on a sampler.

Use the different alphabets (pages 96–103) to customize your sampler, adding names, dates and so on. If you are making it as a gift, add a special message for the recipient.

Work a more elaborate border around the whole design to tie all the elements together. For example, use the beaded border from the Christmas carols on pages 26/27.

To stitch a mirror image of a motif, use a mirror to reflect the image and draw this on graph paper or scan the image into a computer, flip it and print out the new image.

☆ *Stitch for Christmas* ☆

Nativity Sampler

The lovely Nativity Sampler opposite shows how easy it is to create a stunning design using different motifs around a common theme.

Stitch count 139h x 110w

Finished design size 25 x 20cm (10 x 7¾in)

Stitch the sampler over one block of 14-count black Aida using three strands of stranded cotton (floss) for cross stitch. Use one strand for the backstitch outline in 3371 and two strands for all other backstitch. When the stitching is completed, mount into a ready-made frame (see page 16).

Using a Sampler Plan

I used a plan to divide my sampler into sections. Each section on the plan can be made bigger or smaller to accommodate your chosen motifs, but keep the two side panels the same width so the sampler looks balanced. Keeping the bottom border the same height or higher than the top border will look better too.

1 Plan your sampler out on a large sheet of graph paper first. Now draw only the outline of your motifs (there's no need to put colours or details in because when you start stitching you can refer to each chart on its own page). Cut the outlined motifs out to arrange them on the plan.

2 Begin with the centre section and choose something to fill this space. You could use a large motif or a saying or message. The size of this section will dictate the height of the side panels.

3 Add the panels each side and fill these either with several small motifs, one motif repeated or a tall motif. You could use a different idea for each side panel or

stitch the mirror image on the opposite side. The top and bottom panels are the width of the centre section and the two side panels. You could put in a wide motif, several small motifs or one small motif on one side with its mirror image on the other. If you've used a motif in the centre section, you could use the top or bottom panels to add a message.

4 Finally, add a simple border of a line of stitches between the sections; you could work it in metallic thread or beads.

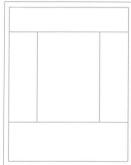

Nativity sampler plan (above)
Two variation sampler plans (right)

Stitching Techniques

This section gives useful advice, especially for beginners, on fabric preparation, how to calculate if you have enough fabric and working the stitches.

Fabrics

The designs have mostly been stitched on Aida fabric where one block corresponds to one square on the chart and one cross stitch is made over one block using the holes as a guide. The designs could also be stitched on an evenweave such as linen but worked over two fabric threads. A design worked on 14-count Aida will be the same size if stitched on 28-count evenweave.

Fabric Size

If you want to frame your design, add at least 15cm (6in) to both measurements of the finished design size. This will give you plenty of fabric to stretch and mount on to a board. If the design is going into card or ready-made item, add at least 7.5cm (3in) to the measurements of the aperture to allow for making up.

Calculating Design Size

Each project gives the stitch count and finished design size but if you plan to work the design on a fabric with a different count, you will need to be able to calculate the finished size.

Work out the finished size of any design by counting the number of stitches in the height of the design and the width of the design and divide these numbers by the fabric count number

For example, this heart bauble has a stitch count of 28h x 23w. The finished size on 14-count Aida would be 28 ÷ 14 = 2in and 23 ÷ 14 = 1.6in (ie, 1½in). So you would need a piece of fabric 2 x 1½in (5 x 4cm), *plus* extra for making up (see above).

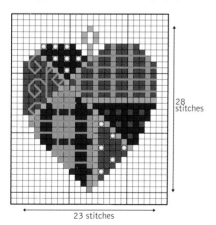

28 stitches

23 stitches

When using aperture cards or ready-made items, measure the aperture or size of the item and compare it with the design size of your chosen motif. If it is too big to fit when worked on 14-count fabric, it will be smaller and may fit if worked on 16-count. Always allow a small margin of fabric between the motif and the aperture so the motif doesn't look as if it has been forced into the space

When working on Aida bands, count the number of stitches on the band width to make sure your design will fit.

Preparing to Stitch

Cut your fabric to size (see Fabric Size, left). To prevent fraying, especially of evenweave fabrics, machine around the edges with a zigzag stitch. To find the centre, fold the fabric in half and then in half again. Place a pin or small tacking stitch where the two folds cross. Press the fabric flat. Place a mark at the centre of the chart. Begin stitching from the middle of the fabric and the middle of the chart to ensure that the design is centred on the fabric.

Using Charts and Keys

The charts in this book are in colour with some colours further identified with black or white symbols.

Each coloured square on the chart represents one cross stitch and each empty square represents unworked fabric. On Aida this is one block and on evenweave it is two threads.

Some designs use three-quarter cross stitches, sometimes called fractional stitches. These are represented by a coloured triangle instead of a coloured square.

For each double-page spread of charts there is a key, which tells you what colours to use. Some pages have their own key, as do some of the larger charts.

Tweeded cross stitch is used to mix metallic threads with the cotton threads. The two colours are listed in the key. Use one strand of each together in the needle.

Backstitch is shown by a coloured line on the chart, with the code given in the key.

French knots are shown by coloured circles and seed beads by larger coloured circles, with all codes given in the key.

DMC threads have been used but you could match the colours to other thread ranges. Exact colour matches are not always possible so check colours carefully.

Washing and Pressing

If your stitching requires washing, hand wash gently in warm water with a non-biological washing powder or liquid. Roll the stitching in a towel to blot off most of the water – never wring. Cover your ironing board with a towel to prevent flattening the stitches, and press the stitching on the wrong side until dry.

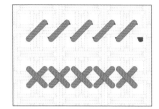

Working the Stitches

Only basic stitches have been used in the designs – all are easy to master and are described here with diagrams.

Starting and Finishing Stitching

It is best to start and finish work neatly in order to avoid a lumpy, uneven look when your work is mounted or framed.

Use a knotless loop start if working with an even number of strands i.e. 2, 4 or 6. To start with two strands, cut the stranded cotton (floss) twice the length that you would normally use. Separate one strand, fold it in half and thread a needle with the two ends. From the wrong side, push the needle up through the fabric where the first stitch is to be, leaving the loop hanging at the back. Form a half cross stitch and pass the needle through the waiting loop. Pull tight and the thread is now anchored. If using four strands, cut two strands of cotton (floss) and fold in half.

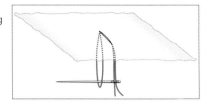

Knotless loop start

Use an away waste knot start if working with an odd number of strands or a tweeded thread. Thread your needle and knot the end. From the front, push the needle down through the fabric about 2.5cm (1in) away from where you want the first stitch to be. Begin the first stitch and work over this thread until it is firmly anchored. Cut off the knot and trim any excess thread neatly.

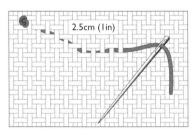

2.5cm (1in)

To finish off thread, pass the needle through some nearby stitches on the wrong side of the work, then cut the thread off close to the fabric. You can also start a new thread in a similar way

Away waste knot start

Backstitch

Backstitches are used to give definition to parts of a design and to outline areas. Many of the charts used different coloured backstitches. To work backstitch, follow the diagram right, bringing the needle up at 1 and down at 2, up again at 3, down at 4 and so on.

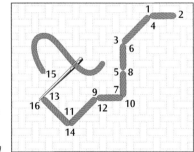

Working backstitch

Cross Stitch

A cross stitch can be worked singly or a number of half stitches can be sewn in a line and completed on the return journey.

To make a cross stitch over one block of Aida (diagram, right), bring the needle up through the fabric at the bottom left side of the stitch (number 1) and cross diagonally to the top left corner (2). Push the needle through the hole and bring up through the bottom right corner (3), crossing the fabric diagonally to the top left corner to finish the stitch (4). To start the next stitch, come up through the bottom left corner of the first stitch.

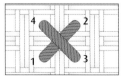

Single cross stitch on Aida fabric

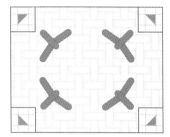

Cross stitch in two journeys on Aida fabric

To work a line of cross stitches, stitch the first part of the stitch as above and repeat these half cross stitches along the row. Complete the crosses on the way back (diagram, left). Note: always finish the cross stitch with the top stitches lying in the same diagonal direction.

Three-quarter Cross Stitch

Three-quarter cross stitches give more detail to a design and can create the illusion of curves. They are shown by a triangle within a square on the charts. If working on Aida, make a quarter stitch from the corner into the centre of the Aida square, piercing the fabric, and then work a half cross stitch across the other diagonal.

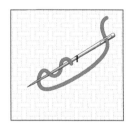

Three-quarter cross stitches

French Knot

French knots are used as full stops in some of the alphabets and as eyes in many designs. To work, follow the diagrams below, bringing the needle and thread up through the fabric at the exact place where the knot is to be positioned. Wrap the thread twice around the needle, holding the thread firmly close to the needle, then twist the needle back through the fabric as close as possible to where it first emerged. Holding the knot down, pull the thread through to the back leaving the knot on the surface, securing it with one small stitch on the back.

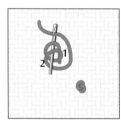

Working a French knot

Using Beads

When using different types of beads than those listed, make sure they will cover the same space as a stitch; too big and they will be out of proportion to the rest of the design, for example, giant berries with tiny holly leaves.

Beads can be attached as part of a cross stitch (see diagram below). Thread the bead on to the needle while working the first part of the cross, and then complete the cross by laying one strand each side of the bead. Bring the needle back up to the front of the fabric, ready to make another stitch or add another bead.

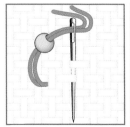
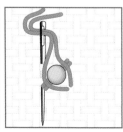

Attaching a bead as part of a cross stitch

Making Up the Projects

This book has photographs displaying some of the designs made up in different ways, and there are plenty of suggestions for other ways to use the motifs. Dip into the Motif Library and use the instructions in this section to create a beautiful selection of Christmas cards, gifts and keepsakes.

Advent Calendar

You will need: backing fabric, thin wadding, 25 small rings, thin ribbon, wider ribbon for hanging loops, length of wooden doweling, two large wooden beads and pins.

1 You will need to work on a piece of Aida 51 x 46cm (20 x 18in). Stitch the first six advent calendar motifs in a row about 9cm (3½in) from the top of the fabric, each motif 1cm (½in) apart (six Aida blocks). Stitch another row of six motifs 3.3cm (1¼in) below (eighteen Aida blocks), making sure they are in line with the first row. Stitch two more rows the same measurement apart. Find the centre of the last row, measure down 3.3cm (1¼in) and work the final motif central to this mark.

2 Trim the finished embroidery into a rectangle, leaving 2.5cm (1in) on side edges and top and 6cm (2¼in) on the bottom edge. Cut a piece of backing fabric the same size. Cut a piece of wadding 1.5cm (⅝in) smaller on all sides. Pin and tack (baste) the wadding to the back of the embroidery, leaving a 1.5cm (⅝in) gap around all edges. Stitch diagonal lines of tacking from corner to corner and around the edges.

3 Place the embroidery and backing fabric right sides together. Stitch together using a seam allowance of 1.5cm (⅝in), leaving the bottom edge open. Turn the calendar through to the right side, pushing the wadding into the corners. Sew the open edge closed.

4 Cut three 7.5cm (3in) lengths of wide ribbon, fold in half and stitch one to the centre of the top edge on the wrong side. Stitch the other two each side 4cm (1½in) in from the side edge.

5 Sew a ring below each motif, stitching through the wadding and backing fabric. Remove the tacking stitches. Cut 25 lengths of the ribbon and tie on to the rings with a knot.

6 Thread the dowelling through the top loops and cut to length. Sharpen each end with a pencil sharpener and add a wooden bead. Attach a piece of wide ribbon as a hanging loop.

Card Hanger

You will need: mount board, four small rings, ribbon, double-sided tape, PVA glue and pins.

1 Measure the embroidery and add 1.5cm (¾in) all around. Cut two pieces of mount board using these measurements and a third piece 1cm (½in) smaller. Stick the two larger pieces of mount board together using double-sided tape.

2 Lay the embroidery right side up on the mount board, making sure the design is central and straight, matching a fabric thread along the edges. Push pins through at the four corners and along the edges to mark the position. Trim the fabric to leave 5cm (2in) all around.

3 Turn the embroidery and mount board over together. Stick double-sided tape around the edges of the board and peel off the backing tape. Fold the excess fabric back, pressing down firmly to stick the fabric to the board, adding more tape to neaten the corners.

4 Cover the back of the smaller piece of mount board with PVA glue and stick to the back of the card hanger, covering the turned-back fabric. Wipe off excess glue and place a weight on to the card hanger to hold in position until the glue dries.

5 Stitch two rings on the top edge of the card hanger and two on the bottom. Make a hanging loop and thread through the top rings, sewing into place. To finish, cut two lengths of ribbon and sew each on to a bottom ring. Attach the cards using small clips or bright paper clips.

Decorations

You will need: felt, medium-weight iron-on interfacing, polyester stuffing (or cloves or pot-pourri) and 13cm (5in) length of ribbon.

1 Fuse the iron-on interfacing to the wrong side of the finished embroidery (see page 12). Trim the embroidery 2cm (¾in) beyond the widest measurements of the design shape.

2 Fold the length of ribbon in half and tack (baste) into the middle of the top edge on the wrong side (or at one corner for the stocking). Cut a piece of felt the same size as the embroidery and pin on to the wrong side of the design.

3 Use two strands of a cotton (floss) colour used in the embroidery to stitch around the edge of the design using neat running stitches (stitch through all thicknesses of the ribbon to secure) but leave a gap on one edge to push the stuffing through. Stuff the decoration, pushing the stuffing into any corners. Sew the open edge closed.

4 Trim around the embroidered shape, leaving two squares of Aida or four threads of evenweave on all edges (don't cut through the ribbon!). Add a tassel at the bottom if desired.

Making a tassel Cut a rectangle of stiff card, about 1.25cm (½in) longer than the desired length of the tassel. Choose a thread from your project and wrap it round the card to the desired thickness. Slip a long length of thread under the strands at the top, fold in half and secure tightly with a knot, leaving two long ends. Cut the wrapped threads at the bottom and remove the card. Thread one long end on to a blunt needle, insert it through the top of the strands and bring out 1.25cm (½in) below. Wrap the long end around the tassel several times, bring the needle back through the top and use the long ends to sew the tassel in place. Trim the bottom neatly.

Heart Garland

You will need: gingham backing fabric, gingham ribbon, string, polyester stuffing, wooden beads, a large-eyed tapestry needle and pins.

1 Once all the stitching is complete, cut out each heart leaving a seam allowance of 1.5cm (⅝in). For each heart, cut a piece of backing fabric the same size and pin together with right sides facing. Stitch the pieces together, leaving a gap along one straight edge.

2 Stuff each heart, pushing the stuffing into the point and then sew the gap closed.

3 Lay the hearts out in order with a bead between. Thread the string on to the needle. Tie a loose knot into the long end

to prevent it being pulled through. Carefully push the needle from left to right through the first heart from the side seam and out the opposite seam. Thread on a bead and repeat until all the hearts are threaded on the string (see the picture on page 5).

4 Space the hearts and beads out evenly. Tie a length of gingham ribbon to each end of the string, tightening the knot close to the heart.

Peace, Joy and Love Angels

Angel card Back the embroidery with double-sided iron-on interfacing (see page 12). Trim the Aida to within three squares of the embroidery. Cut a piece of gingham fabric bigger than the card aperture. Place the embroidery in the middle of the fabric and fuse together. Overcast the edge of the embroidery using two strands of a cotton used in the design. Mount the design into the aperture card (see page 10).

Angel gift bag Trim the Aida to within six squares of the embroidery. Cut a piece of felt 2.5cm (1in) larger on all sides. Stitch the embroidery on to the felt using two strands of a

cotton used in the design. Work a second line of stitching in another colour. Using double-sided tape, stick the patch on to a ready-made gift bag.

Angel decoration Follow steps 1 to 4 of the decorations, above. Use stranded cotton to make a hanging loop at the top and to tie on two bells and a wooden heart at the bottom.

DMC stranded cotton
Cross stitch

• blanc	414	742	− 793	3820	
⁄ ecru	415	○ 743	815	3822	
153	550	↑ 745	904	∧ 3852 + E3852	
304	V 553	− 783	✕ 906	(1 strand of each)	
L 318	666	• 791	907	Backstitch	
U 347	I 740	792	＼ 3078	— 869	

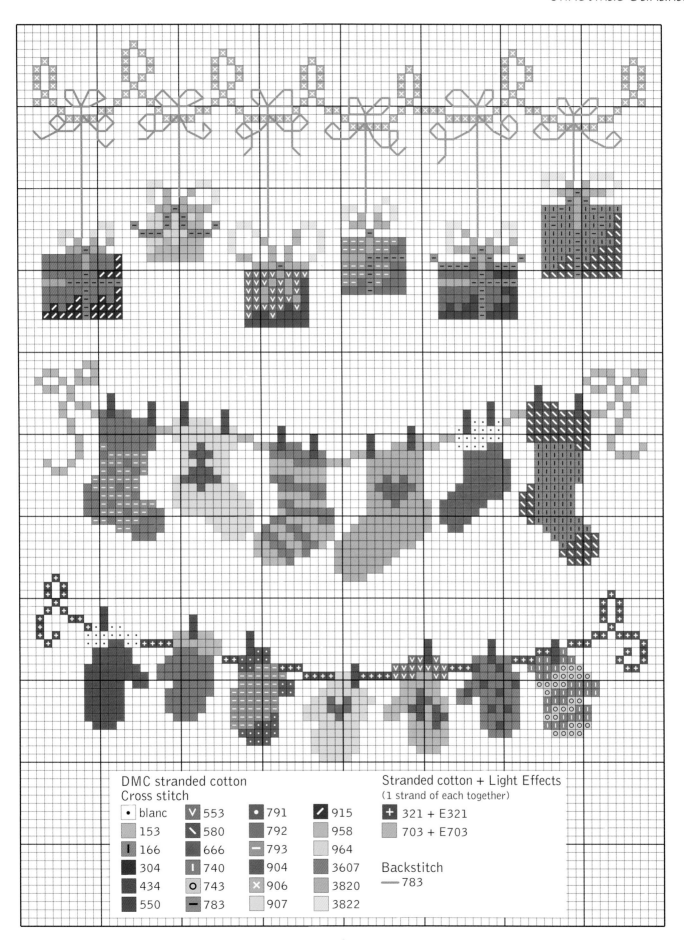

DMC stranded cotton
Cross stitch

• blanc	V 553	• 791	/ 915
153	\ 580	792	958
I 166	666	— 793	964
304	I 740	904	3607
434	o 743	× 906	3820
550	— 783	907	3822

Stranded cotton + Light Effects
(1 strand of each together)

+ 321 + E321

703 + E703

Backstitch
—— 783

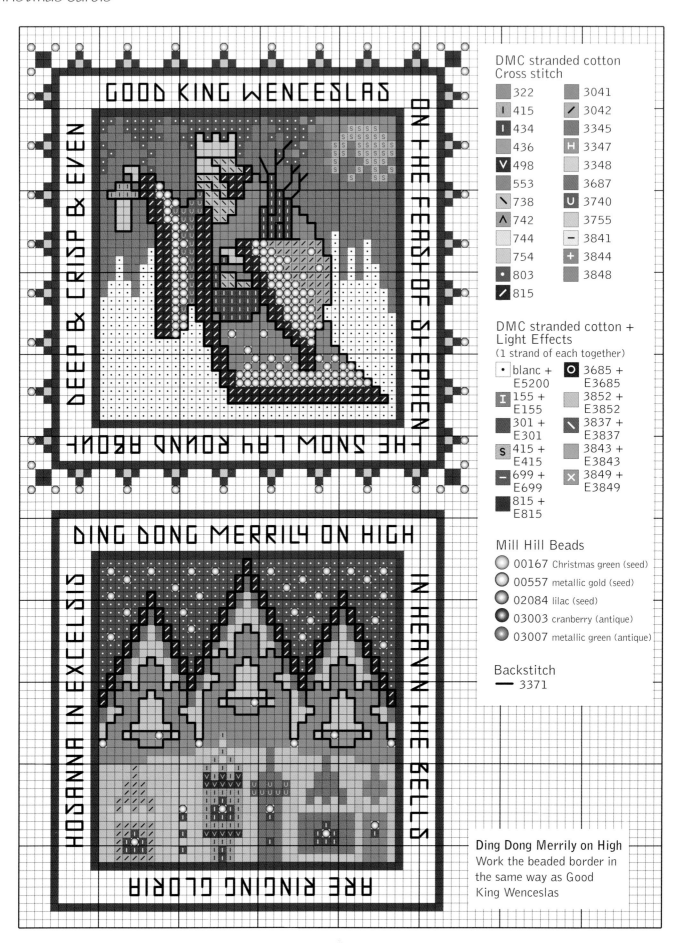

The Holly and the Ivy
Work the beaded border in the same way as We Three Kings

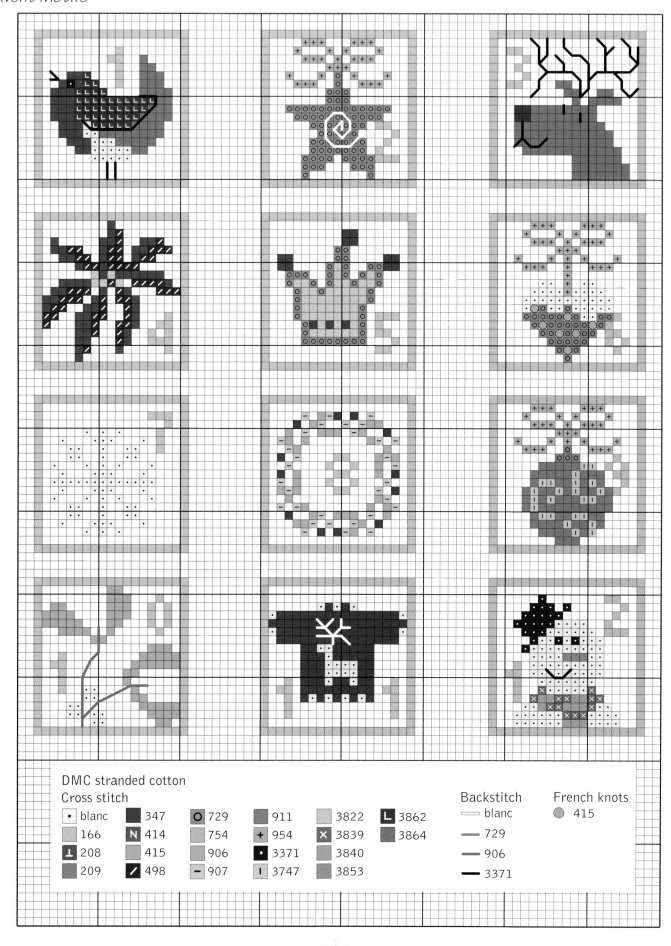

DMC stranded cotton
Cross stitch

• blanc	347	O 729	911	3822	L 3862
166	N 414	754	+ 954	X 3839	3864
⊥ 208	415	906	⊙ 3371	3840	
209	╱ 498	– 907	I 3747	3853	

Backstitch
— blanc
— 729
— 906
— 3371

French knots
● 415

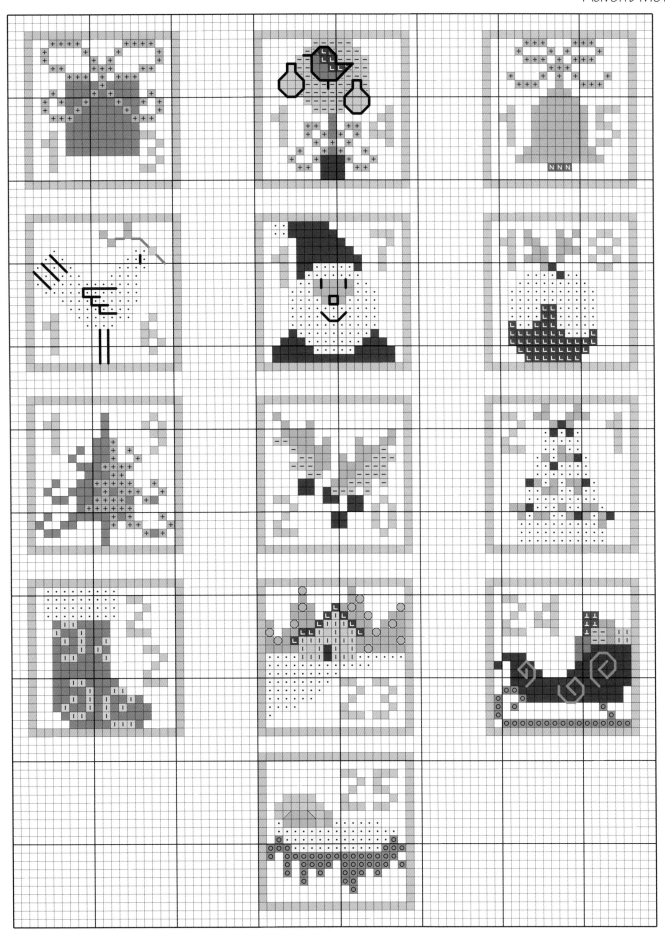

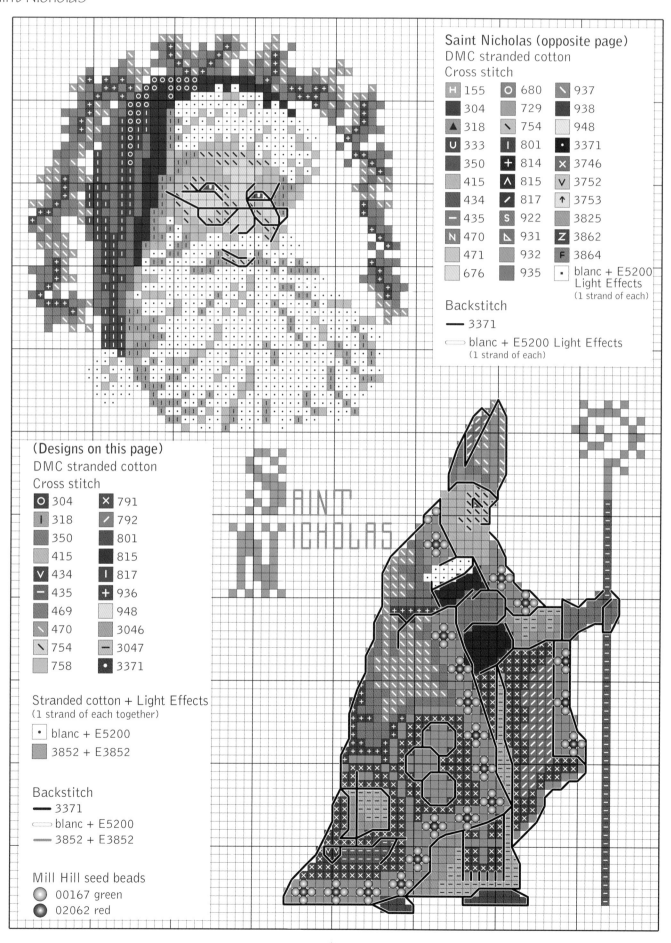

Saint Nicholas (opposite page)
DMC stranded cotton
Cross stitch

H	155	O	680	╲	937
■	304		729	╲	938
▲	318	╲	754		948
U	333	I	801	•	3371
■	350	+	814	X	3746
∧	415	∧	815	V	3752
	434	╱	817	↑	3753
–	435	S	922		3825
N	470	∟	931	Z	3862
	471		932	F	3864
	676		935	•	blanc + E5200 Light Effects (1 strand of each)

Backstitch

— 3371

⊂⊃ blanc + E5200 Light Effects
(1 strand of each)

(Designs on this page)
DMC stranded cotton
Cross stitch

O	304	X	791
I	318	╱	792
	350		801
	415	■	815
V	434	I	817
–	435	+	936
	469		948
╲	470		3046
╲	754	–	3047
	758	•	3371

Stranded cotton + Light Effects
(1 strand of each together)

• blanc + E5200

■ 3852 + E3852

Backstitch

— 3371

⊂⊃ blanc + E5200

— 3852 + E3852

Mill Hill seed beads

○ 00167 green

● 02062 red

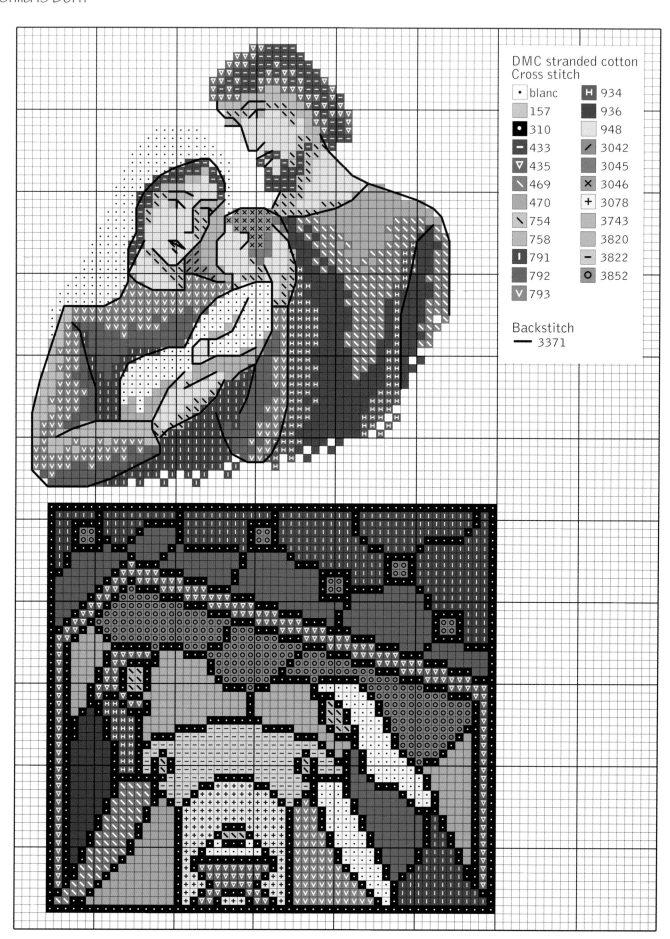

DMC stranded cotton
Cross stitch

•	blanc	H	934
	157		936
●	310		948
−	433	╱	3042
▽	435		3045
╲	469	✕	3046
	470	+	3078
╲	754		3743
	758		3820
I	791	−	3822
	792	O	3852
V	793		

Backstitch
— 3371

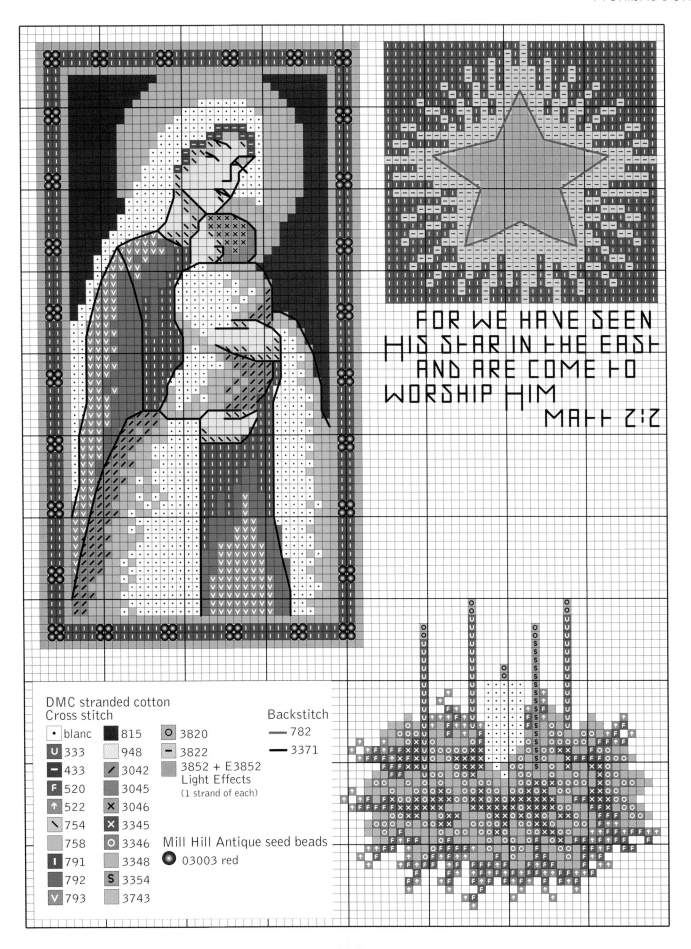

FOR WE HAVE SEEN
HIS STAR IN THE EAST
AND ARE COME TO
WORSHIP HIM
MATT 2:2

DMC stranded cotton
Cross stitch

- blanc
- U 333
- ─ 433
- F 520
- ↑ 522
- \ 754
- 758
- I 791
- 792
- V 793
- 815
- 948
- / 3042
- 3045
- × 3046
- × 3345
- O 3346
- 3348
- S 3354
- 3743
- O 3820
- − 3822
- 3852 + E3852
  Light Effects
  (1 strand of each)

Backstitch
— 782
— 3371

Mill Hill Antique seed beads
● 03003 red

DMC stranded cotton
Cross stitch

•	blanc	◖	938
╱	162	L	986
+	209		988
	321		3041
∧	434	−	3685
╲	720		3688
O	816	T	3740
	904		3837
I	906		3852
	907		

Backstitch
— blanc
— 904
— 938

French knots
● 720 ● 938

34

merry

Yuletide

Snowmen

have warm hearts

Left half of chart

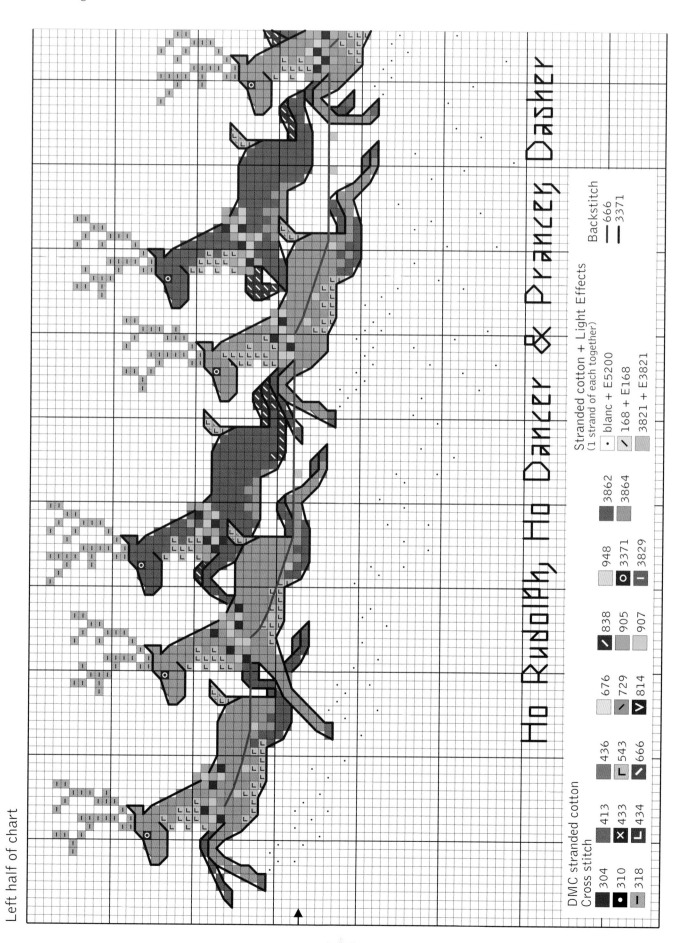

Ho Rudolph, Ho Dancer & Dancer & Prancer Dasher

Backstitch
— 666
— 3371

Stranded cotton + Light Effects
(1 strand of each together)
· blanc + E5200
/ 168 + E168
▨ 3821 + E3821

3862
3864

838   948
905   3371
907   3829

676   814
729
666

DMC stranded cotton
Cross stitch

304   413   436
310   433   543
318   434   666

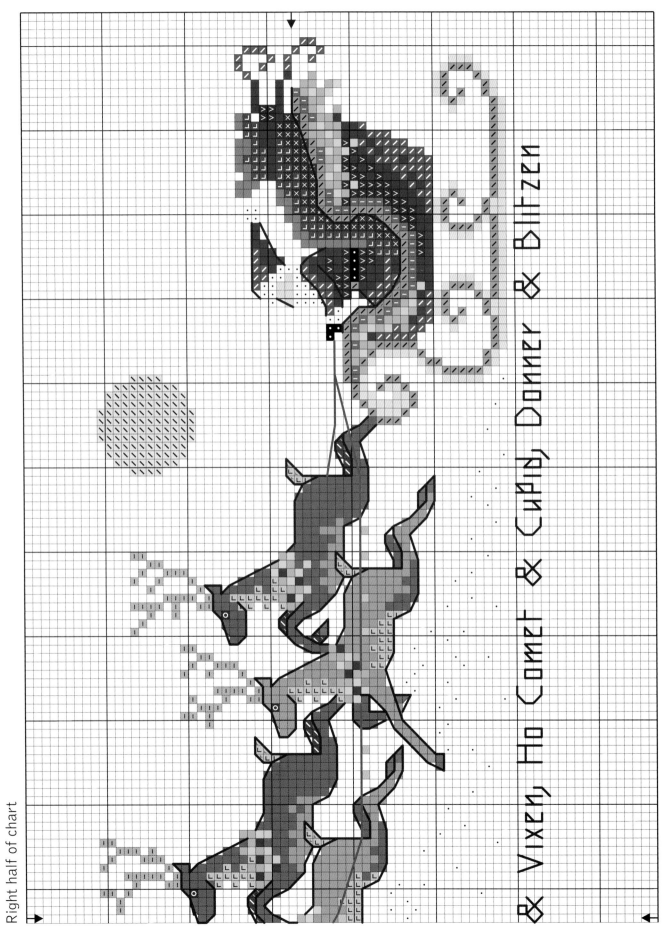

Right half of chart

& Vixen, Ho Comet & Cupid, Donner & Blitzen

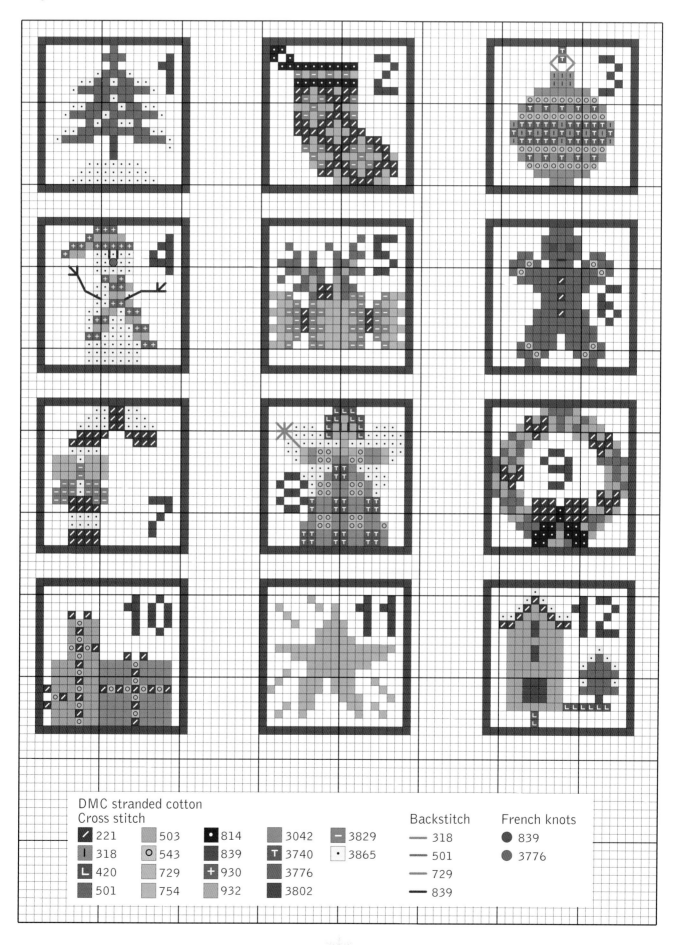

DMC stranded cotton
Cross stitch

/	221		503	•	814		3042	–	3829
I	318	O	543		839	T	3740	•	3865
L	420		729	+	930		3776		
	501		754		932		3802		

Backstitch
— 318
— 501
— 729
— 839

French knots
● 839
● 3776

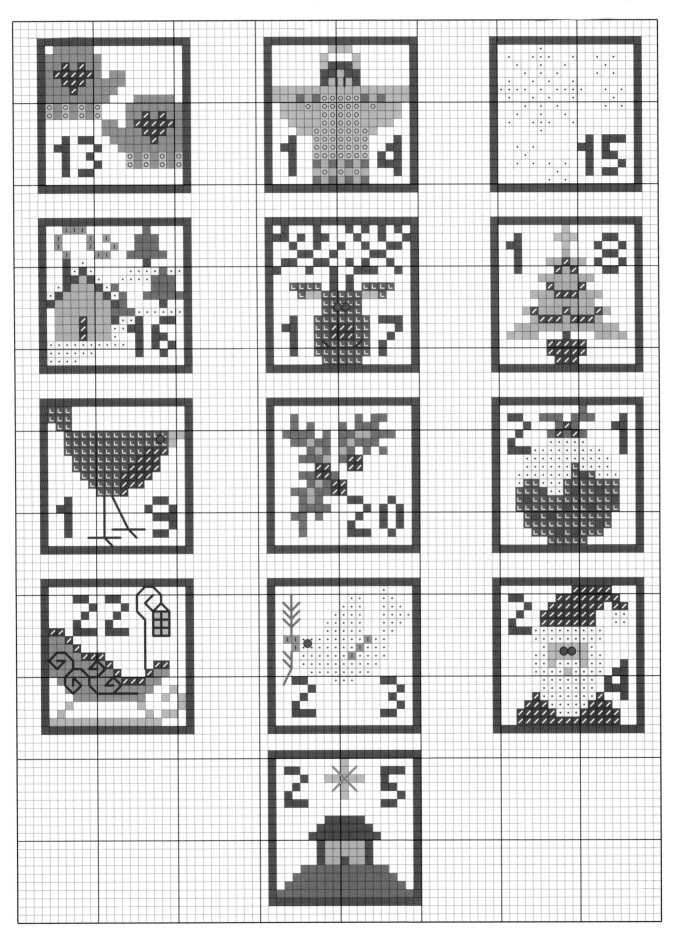

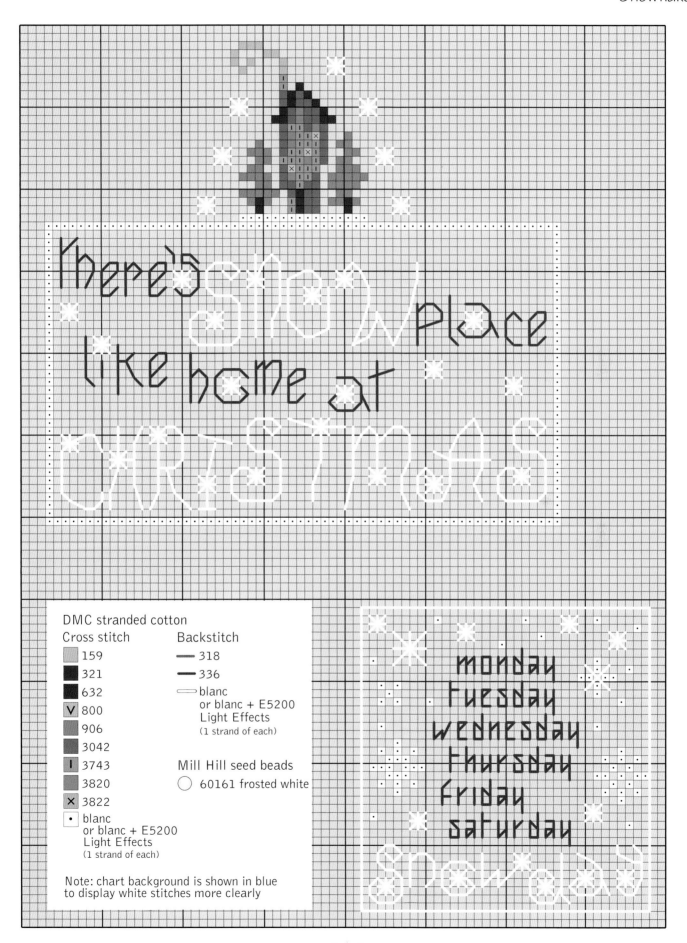

DMC stranded cotton

Cross stitch

- 159
- 321
- 632
- V 800
- 906
- 3042
- I 3743
- 3820
- X 3822
- • blanc
  or blanc + E5200
  Light Effects
  (1 strand of each)

Backstitch

- —— 318
- —— 336
- ⊂⊃ blanc
  or blanc + E5200
  Light Effects
  (1 strand of each)

Mill Hill seed beads

- ◯ 60161 frosted white

Note: chart background is shown in blue
to display white stitches more clearly

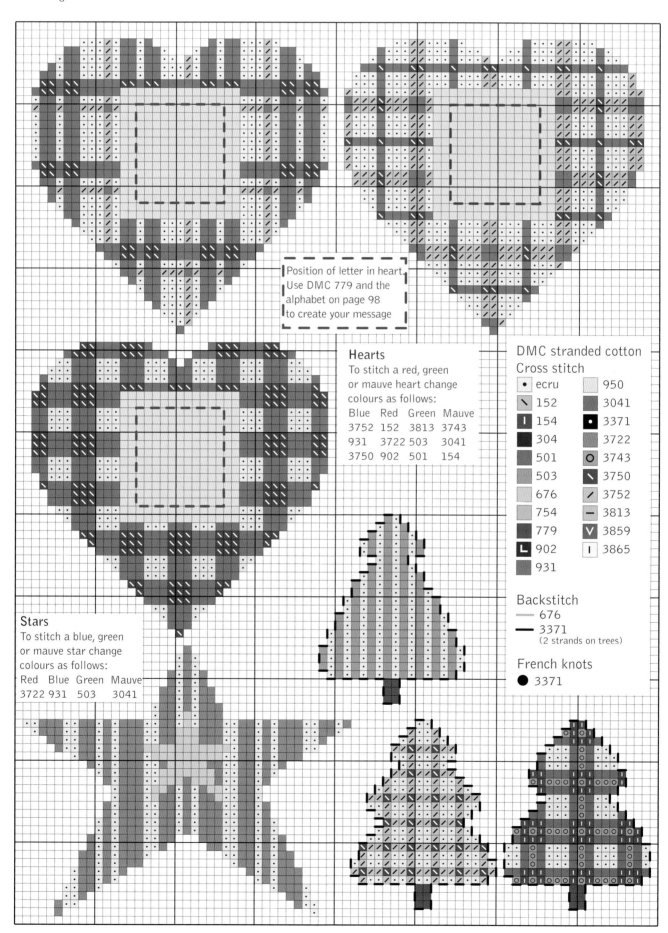

Position of letter in heart.
Use DMC 779 and the
alphabet on page 98
to create your message

Hearts
To stitch a red, green
or mauve heart change
colours as follows:

Blue	Red	Green	Mauve
3752	152	3813	3743
931	3722	503	3041
3750	902	501	154

Stars
To stitch a blue, green
or mauve star change
colours as follows:

Red	Blue	Green	Mauve
3722	931	503	3041

**DMC stranded cotton
Cross stitch**

•	ecru		950
\	152		3041
I	154	•	3371
	304		3722
	501	O	3743
	503	\	3750
	676	/	3752
	754	−	3813
	779	V	3859
L	902	I	3865
	931		

Backstitch
— 676
— 3371
(2 strands on trees)

French knots
● 3371

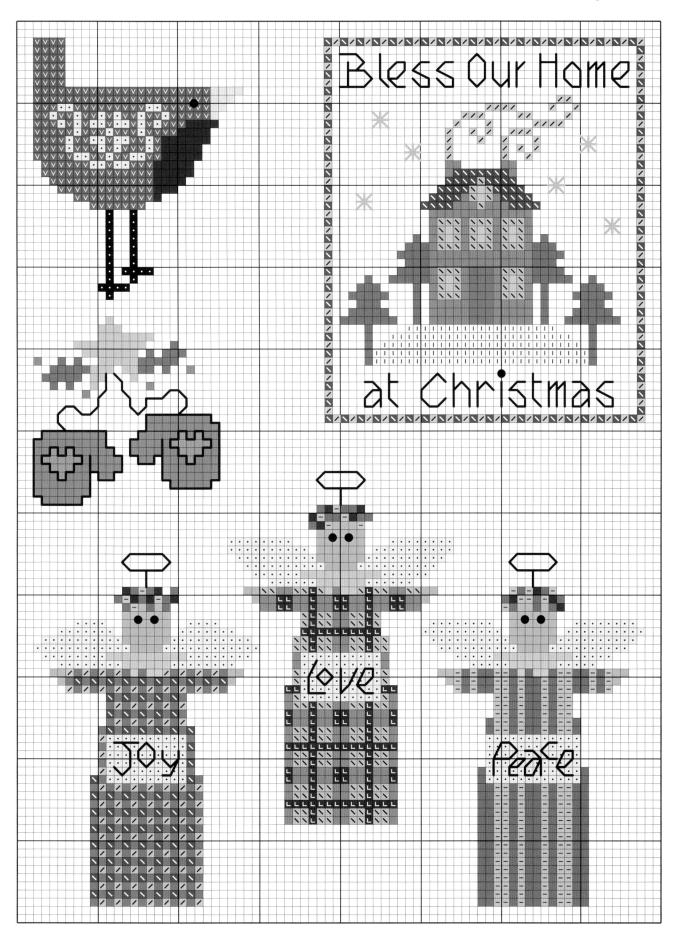

Bless Our Home

at Christmas

Joy

Love

Peace

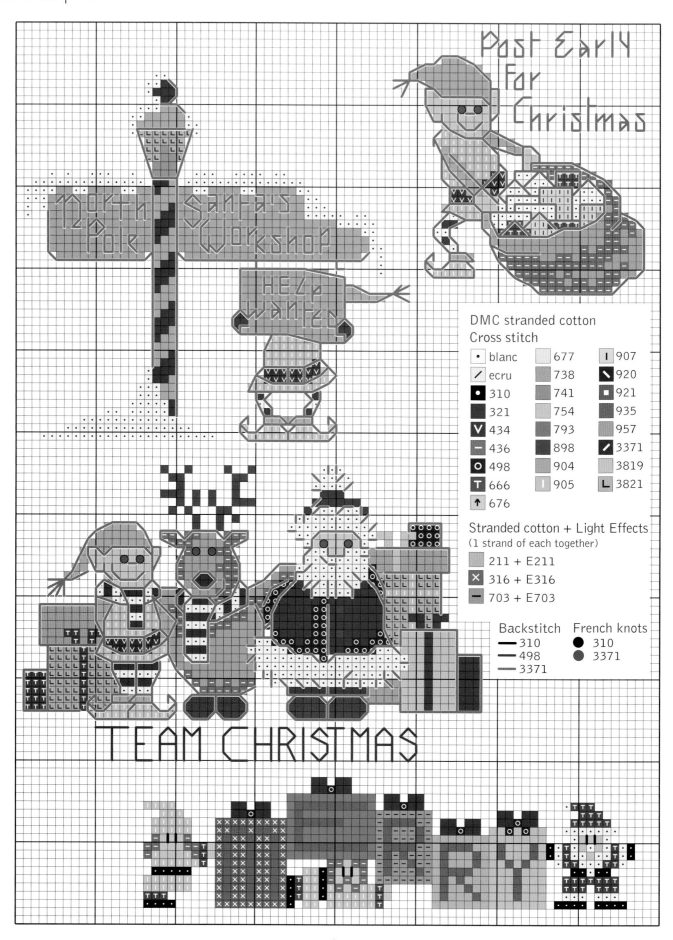

DMC stranded cotton
Cross stitch

· blanc		677	I	907
/ ecru		738	\	920
· 310		741	□	921
321		754		935
V 434		793		957
– 436		898	/	3371
O 498		904		3819
T 666	I	905	L	3821
↑ 676				

Stranded cotton + Light Effects
(1 strand of each together)

	211 + E211
×	316 + E316
–	703 + E703

Backstitch
— 310
— 498
— 3371

French knots
● 310
● 3371

He knows if you've been Bad or Good

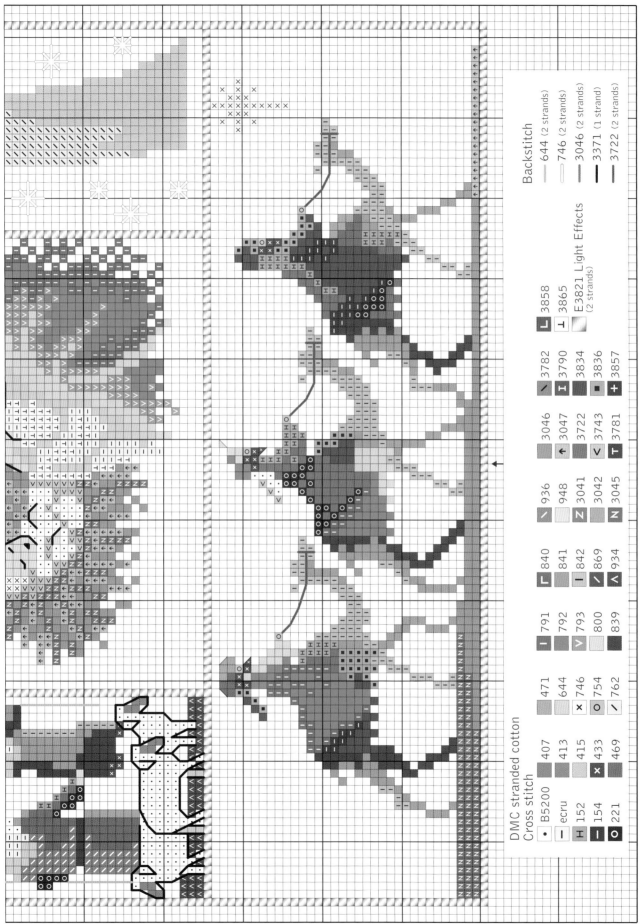

Backstitch

	644 (2 strands)
	746 (2 strands)
	3046 (2 strands)
	3371 (1 strand)
	3722 (2 strands)

| L | 3858 |
| T | 3865 |

E3821 Light Effects (2 strands)

| / | 3782 | I | 3790 | | 3834 |
| | 3836 | + | 3857 | | |

| | 3046 | ← | 3047 | | 3722 |
| V | 3743 | T | 3781 | | |

| | 936 | | 948 | Z | 3041 |
| · | 3042 | N | 3045 | | |

| L | 840 | | 841 | I | 842 |
| / | 869 | ∧ | 934 | | |

| I | 791 | | 792 | V | 793 |
| | 800 | | 839 | | |

| | 471 | | 644 | × | 746 |
| O | 754 | / | 762 | | |

DMC stranded cotton
Cross stitch

·	B5200		407		413
H	415	×	433	I	469
O	221				

DANCER&
PRANCER
DASHER
&VIXEN
COMET
&CUPID
DONNER
&BLITZEN
RUDOLPH

Rudolph

Reindeer Games Played Here

DMC stranded cotton
Cross stitch

· blanc
/ ecru
  318
\ 321
| 434
  436
+ 543
  666
  729
  801
■ 3371
– 3862
  3864
  E3852
  Light Effects

Backstitch
—— 3371
—— E3852
  Light Effects

French knots
● 3371
○ E3852
  Light Effects

DMC stranded cotton

Cross stitch

- · blanc
- / ecru
- T 154
- ▲ 300
- 318
- ↘ 321
- O 347
- 400
- I 434
- 469
- 666
- 676
- V 680
- 729
- 747
- 754
- L 762
- 801
- 932
- 935
- ✕ 3345
- 3347
- ⊡ 3371
- 3750
- 3834
- — 3862
- 3864
- ◩ E3852
  Light Effects

Backstitch

- —— 321
- —— 3347
- —— 3371

French knots

- ● 3371

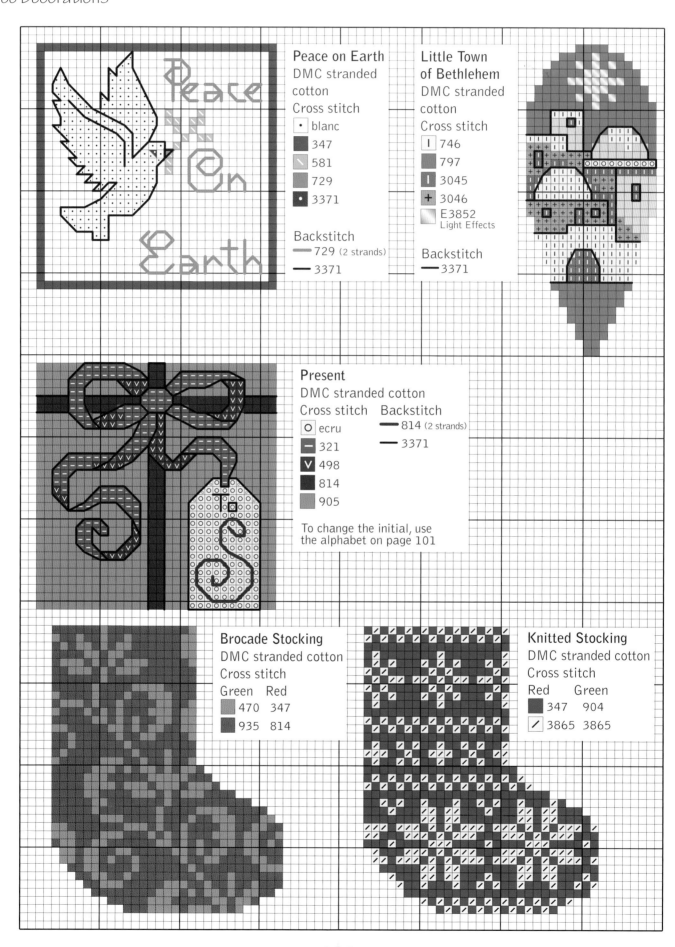

Peace on Earth
DMC stranded cotton
Cross stitch
- · blanc
- 347
- 581
- 729
- · 3371

Backstitch
— 729 (2 strands)
— 3371

Little Town of Bethlehem
DMC stranded cotton
Cross stitch
- I 746
- 797
- I 3045
- + 3046
- E3852 Light Effects

Backstitch
— 3371

Present
DMC stranded cotton
Cross stitch   Backstitch
- O ecru   — 814 (2 strands)
- – 321   — 3371
- V 498
- 814
- 905

To change the initial, use the alphabet on page 101

Brocade Stocking
DMC stranded cotton
Cross stitch
Green Red
- 470   347
- 935   814

Knitted Stocking
DMC stranded cotton
Cross stitch
Red   Green
- 347   904
- / 3865 3865

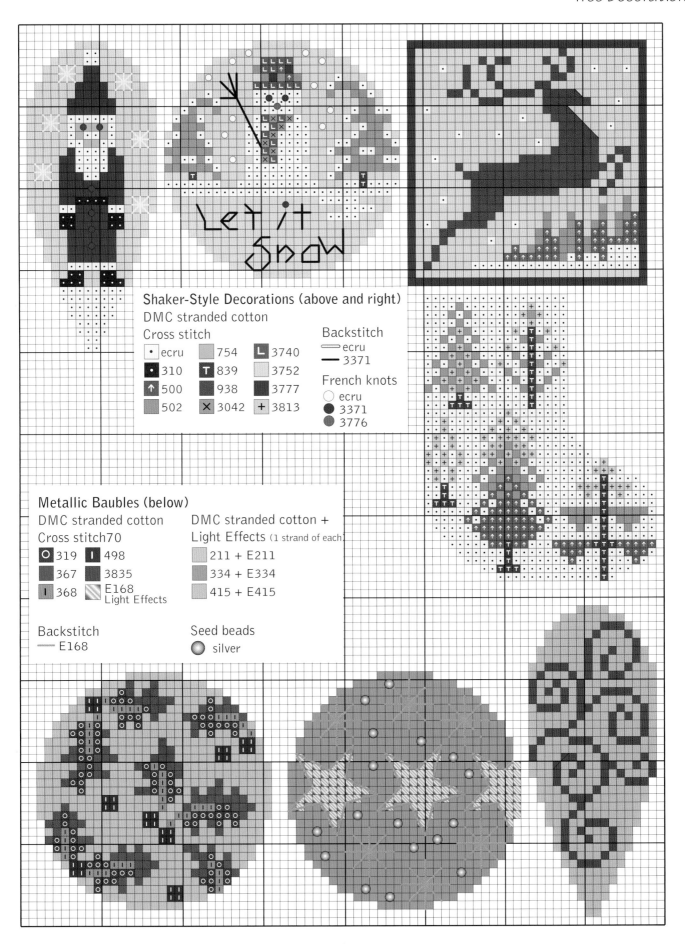

Let it Snow

Shaker-Style Decorations (above and right)
DMC stranded cotton

Cross stitch
- · ecru
- ● 310
- ↑ 500
- ▨ 502
- ▨ 754
- T 839
- ▨ 938
- ✕ 3042
- L 3740
- ▨ 3752
- ▨ 3777
- + 3813

Backstitch
- ═ ecru
- ── 3371

French knots
- ○ ecru
- ● 3371
- ● 3776

Metallic Baubles (below)
DMC stranded cotton

Cross stitch 70
- ◉ 319
- ▨ 367
- ▯ 368
- ▮ 498
- ▨ 3835
- ▨ E168 Light Effects

DMC stranded cotton + Light Effects (1 strand of each)
- ▨ 211 + E211
- ▨ 334 + E334
- ▨ 415 + E415

Backstitch
- ── E168

Seed beads
- ○ silver

DMC stranded cotton
Cross stitch

•	blanc	∧	522
	151	→	543
I	162	*	741
×	211		743
	318	O	745
–	319	•	791
	321		794
\	353		898
/	355	T	930
+	356	F	931
↑	369		3743
/	415		3752
\	435		3807
	471	L	3862
S	472	–	3864
	520		

Stranded cotton +
Light Effects
(1 strand of each together)

/	blanc + E5200
U	415 + E415

Backstitch
— 3371
⸺ 415 + E415

French knot
● 898

Continue with the row of houses chart on opposite page

52

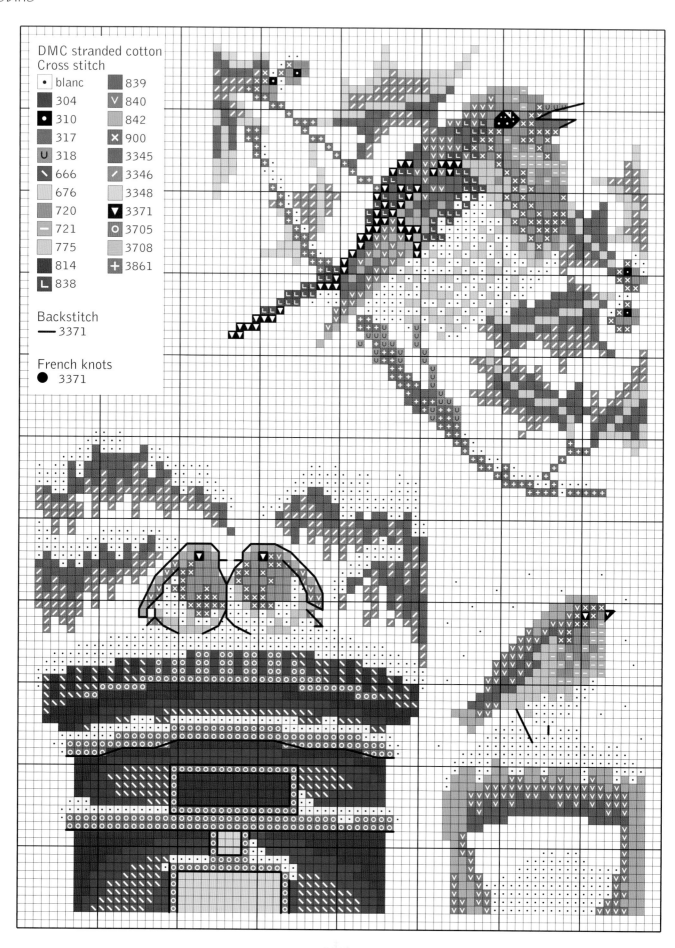

DMC stranded cotton
Cross stitch

•	blanc		839
	304	V	840
•	310		842
	317	✕	900
U	318	／	3345
＼	666	／	3346
	676		3348
	720	▼	3371
─	721	O	3705
	775		3708
	814	＋	3861
L	838		

Backstitch
—— 3371

French knots
● 3371

eat, drink & be merry
'cos it's bird seed tomorrow

tis the season of

Peace & Love

HAPPINESS IS
A WARM
MINCE PIE

Christmas Dawn Chorus

DMC stranded cotton
Cross stitch

Backstitch

- B5200
- 433
- 948
- 3834
- —— 3045
- I 154
- — 435
- 3045
- / 3835
- —— 3371
- O 318
- U 437
- X 3046
- 415
- L 754
- 3047

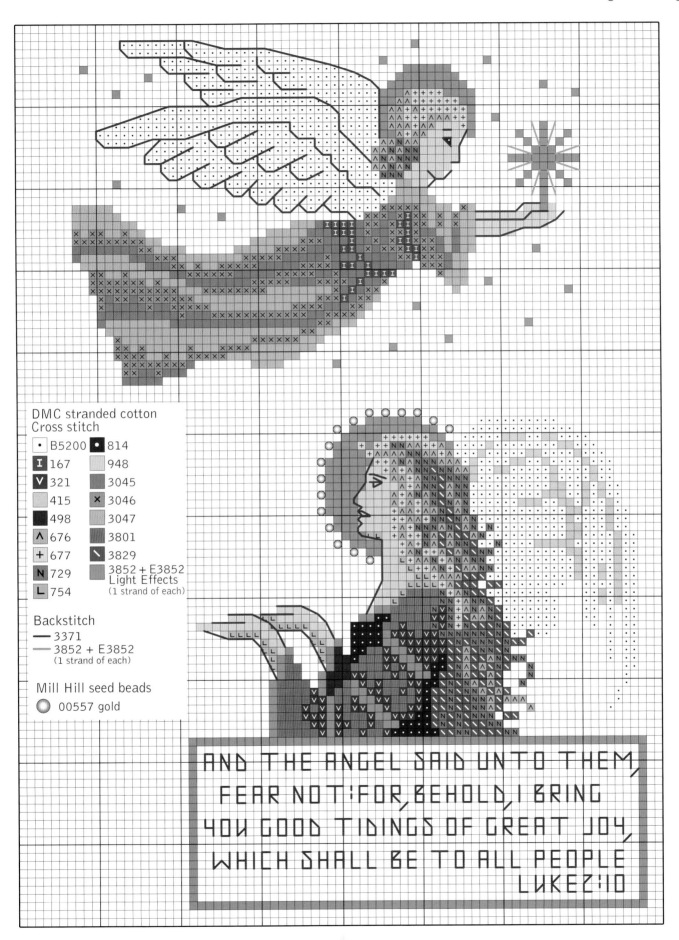

DMC stranded cotton
Cross stitch

- B5200   ● 814
I 167   948
V 321   3045
  415   × 3046
  498   3047
∧ 676   3801
+ 677   3829
N 729   3852 + E3852
L 754   Light Effects
         (1 strand of each)

Backstitch
— 3371
— 3852 + E3852
   (1 strand of each)

Mill Hill seed beads
○ 00557 gold

AND THE ANGEL SAID UNTO THEM,
FEAR NOT;FOR,BEHOLD,I BRING
YOU GOOD TIDINGS OF GREAT JOY,
WHICH SHALL BE TO ALL PEOPLE
LUKE2:10

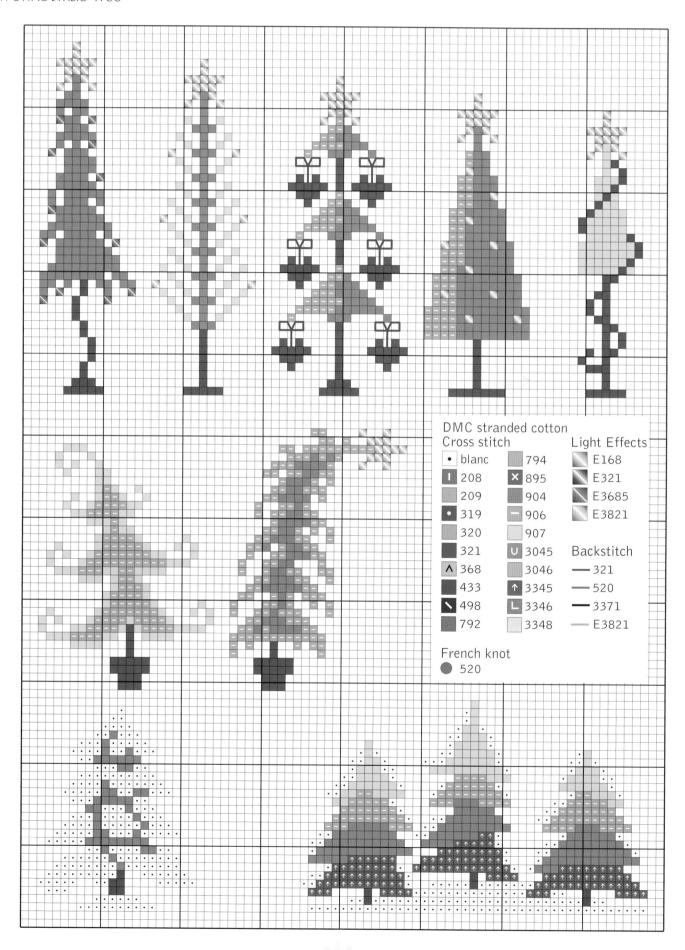

DMC stranded cotton
Cross stitch

•	blanc
I	208
	209
•	319
	320
	321
∧	368
	433
\	498
	792

	794
✗	895
	904
−	906
	907
U	3045
	3046
↑	3345
L	3346
	3348

Light Effects

	E168
	E321
	E3685
	E3821

Backstitch

—	321
—	520
—	3371
—	E3821

French knot
● 520

Change the number using the chart on page 99

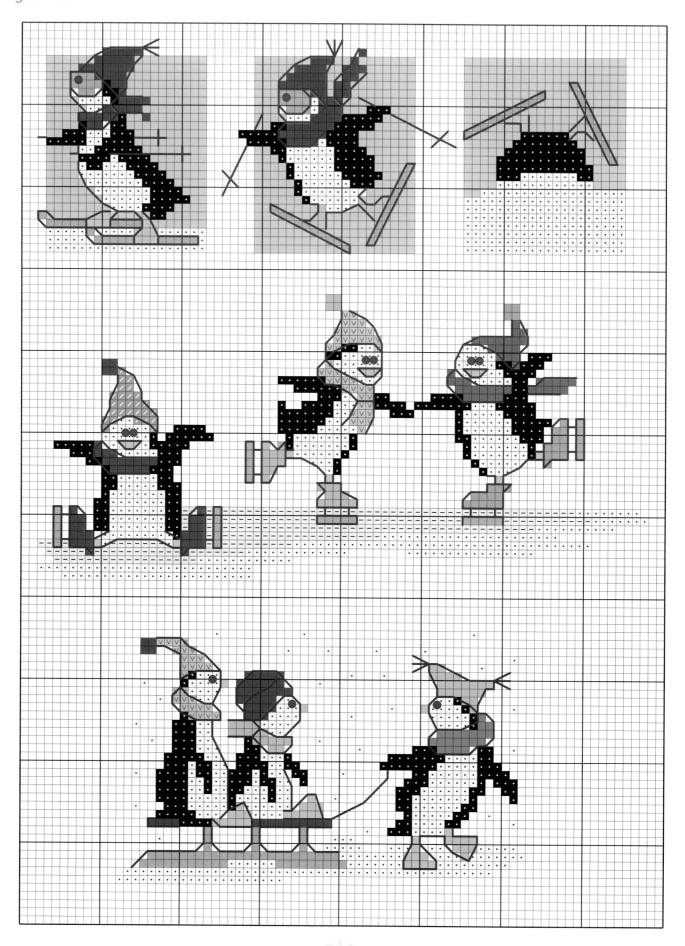

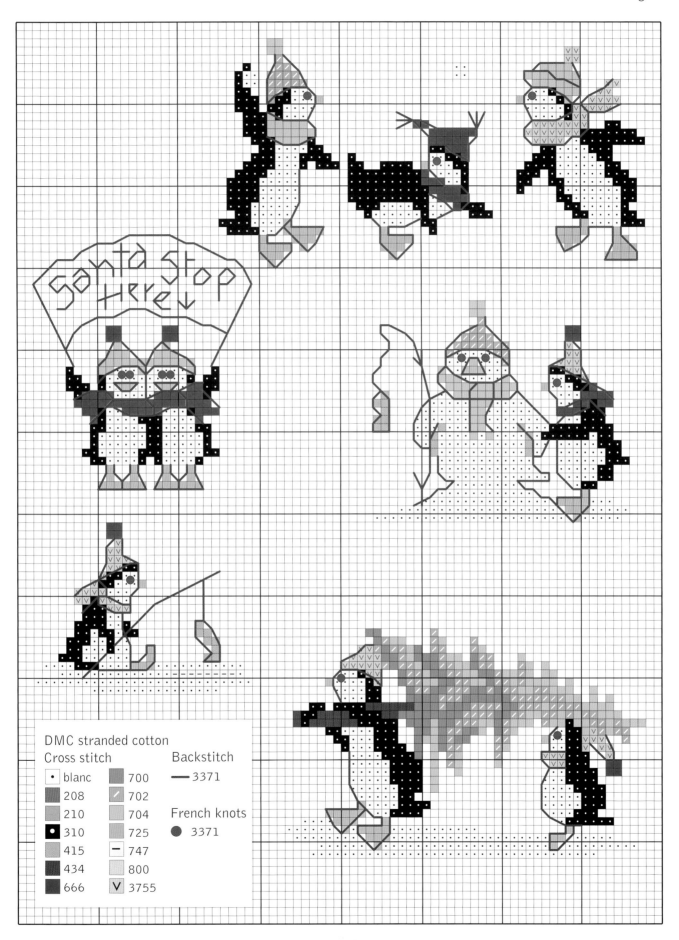

DMC stranded cotton

Cross stitch

- blanc
- 208
- 210
- 310
- 415
- 434
- 666
- 700
- 702
- 704
- 725
- − 747
- 800
- V 3755

Backstitch

— 3371

French knots

● 3371

Teddy's First

Christmas

my First

Christmas Dinner

Baby's First Christmas

Grandma's

Little Star

Santa's Little Helper

Baby's First Christmas Presents

DMC stranded cotton
Cross stitch

• blanc	U 676	◉ 760
V 157	677	/ 794
209	700	800
211	703	/ 898
◉ 310	− 729	\ 963
318	738	3371
434	I 741	3807
\ 436	743	3829
∧ 498	+ 745	
666	754	

Light Effects

E168
E3821

Backstitch

— 3371
— 3807
— E3821

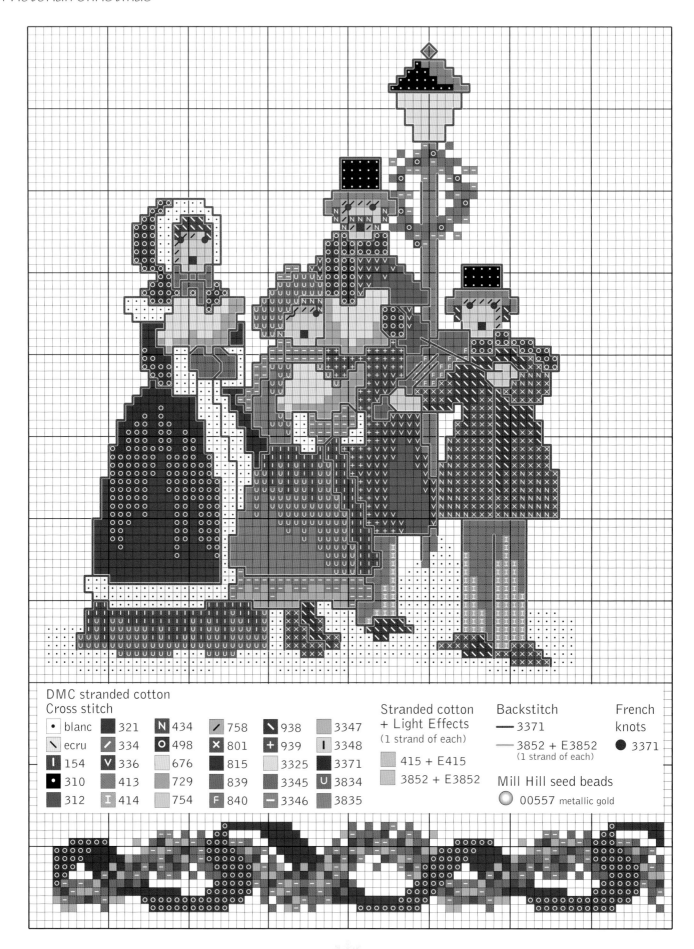

DMC stranded cotton
Cross stitch

• blanc	321	N 434	/ 758	\ 938	3347
\ ecru	/ 334	O 498	X 801	+ 939	I 3348
I 154	V 336	676	815	3325	3371
310	413	729	839	3345	U 3834
312	I 414	754	F 840	− 3346	3835

Stranded cotton + Light Effects
(1 strand of each)

415 + E415
3852 + E3852

Backstitch
— 3371
— 3852 + E3852
(1 strand of each)

French knots
● 3371

Mill Hill seed beads
◯ 00557 metallic gold

Stitch the garland border
charted here and on the
opposite page and repeat
to the length desired

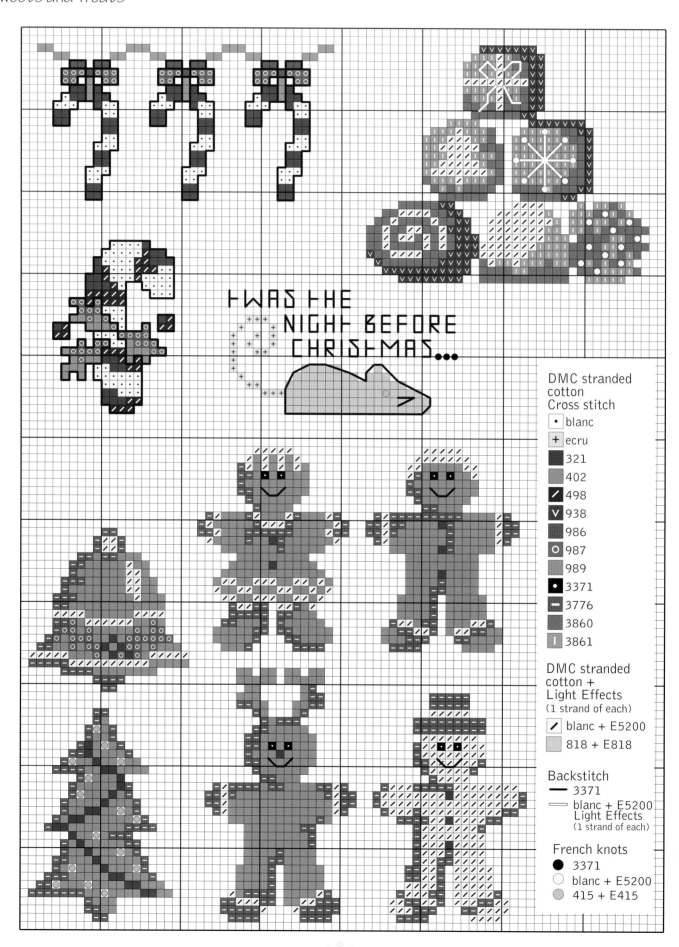

I WAS THE NIGHT BEFORE CHRISTMAS...

DMC stranded cotton
Cross stitch

- • blanc
- + ecru
- ■ 321
- ■ 402
- ◪ 498
- ▼ 938
- ■ 986
- ◉ 987
- ■ 989
- ◨ 3371
- ▬ 3776
- ■ 3860
- ❚ 3861

DMC stranded cotton +
Light Effects
(1 strand of each)

- ◪ blanc + E5200
- ■ 818 + E818

Backstitch
— 3371
═ blanc + E5200
Light Effects
(1 strand of each)

French knots
- ● 3371
- ○ blanc + E5200
- ● 415 + E415

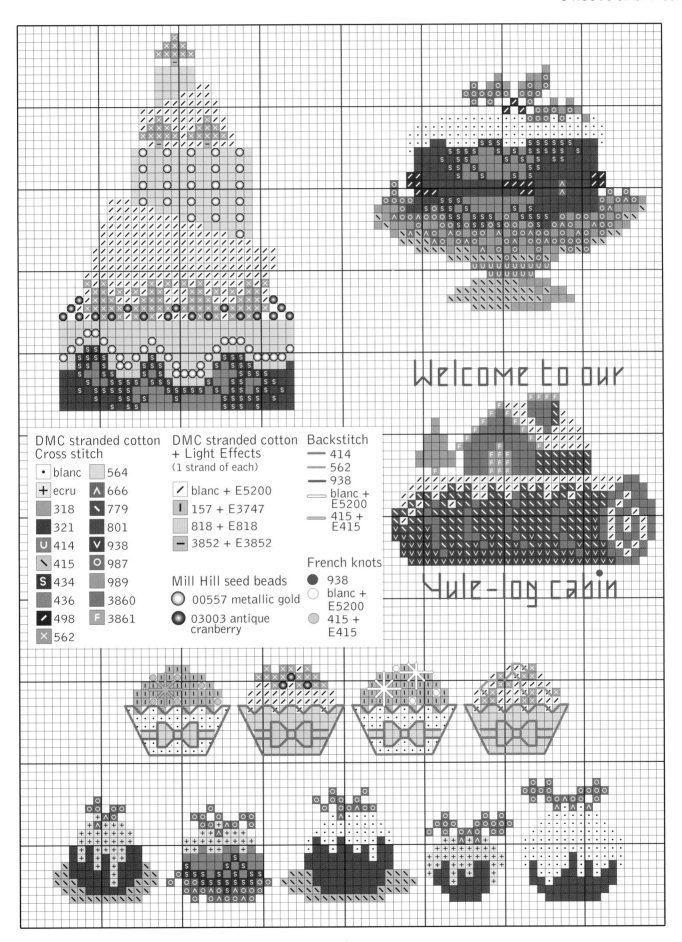

DMC stranded cotton
Cross stitch

- blanc
+ ecru
318
321
U 414
\ 415
S 434
436
/ 498
X 562
564
∧ 666
\ 779
801
V 938
O 987
989
3860
F 3861

DMC stranded cotton
+ Light Effects
(1 strand of each)

/ blanc + E5200
I 157 + E3747
818 + E818
− 3852 + E3852

Mill Hill seed beads
◯ 00557 metallic gold
● 03003 antique cranberry

Backstitch
— 414
— 562
— 938
— blanc + E5200
— 415 + E415

French knots
● 938
◯ blanc + E5200
● 415 + E415

Welcome to our

Yule-log cabin

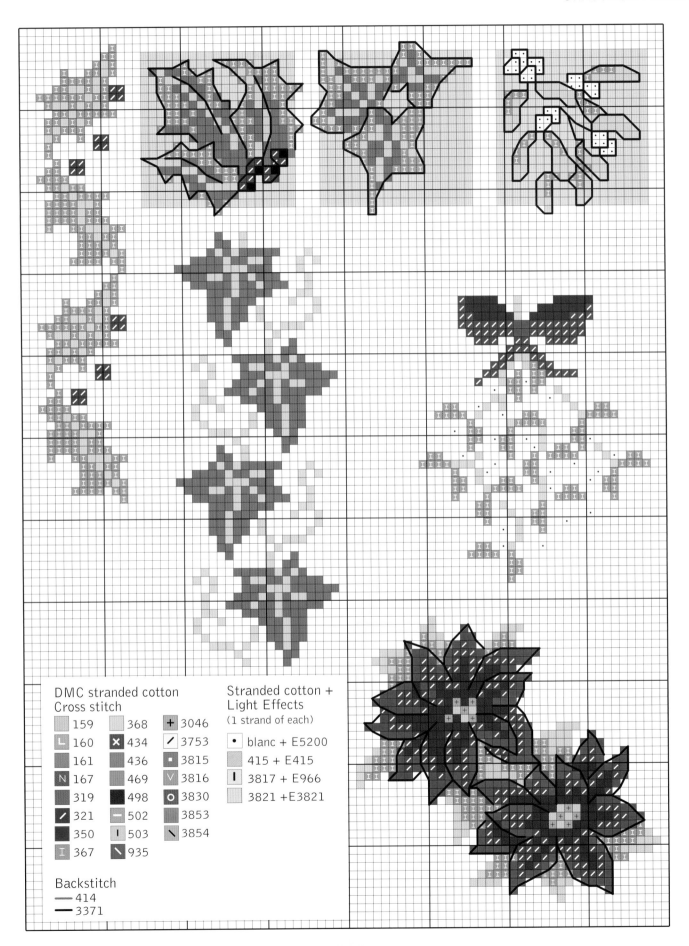

DMC stranded cotton
Cross stitch

159	368	+ 3046
L 160	X 434	/ 3753
161	436	▪ 3815
N 167	469	V 3816
319	498	O 3830
/ 321	− 502	3853
350	I 503	\ 3854
I 367	\ 935	

Stranded cotton +
Light Effects
(1 strand of each)

• blanc + E5200
415 + E415
I 3817 + E966
3821 + E3821

Backstitch
— 414
— 3371

DMC stranded cotton

Cross stitch

•	blanc
V	304
\	602
	603
O	605
	666
	676
	754
•	815
	842
	3371
/	605 + E818 Light Effects (1 strand of each)

Backstitch

▭	blanc
▬	3371

French knots

●	3371

Is it too late

to be good?

Dear Santa
this Christmas
I would like
a bike
a skateboard
a yeti
thank you

Is it too late

to be good?

Dear Santa
this Christmas
I would like
a pink necklace
a pink rabbit
a fairy (any colour)
thank you

DMC stranded cotton
Cross stitch

				Backstitch	French knots
• blanc	✕ 729	∩ 842	■ 3371	— 3371	● 3371
V 304	744	– 905	3807		
415	754	I 932	3821 + E3821 Light Effects (1 strand of each)		
434	794	\ 3064			
666	• 815	3345			
676	841	+ 3347			

Do not open til Christmas

From Your Secret Santa

DIRECT FROM The North Pole

some extra Christmas sparkle!

a gift from Santa xx

I wish you a warm & cosy Christmas

Sent across the miles with Love

DMC stranded cotton
Cross stitch

- blanc
/ 157
▨ 321
415
553
554
741
O 742
\ 744

754
× 783
793
− 816
839
\ 904
906
■ 3371
I 3776

■ 3820
3822
U 3859
V 3821 + E3821
Light Effects
(1 strand of each)

Backstitch
⬭ blanc
— 321
906
— 3371
3821 + E3821

French knots
● 3371

handmade with love

Knit with Love

Knitted crocheted stitched just for you

MADE WITH Love x

From my Kitchen to you

Made with Christmas Spirit

poinsettia fairy

present fairy

christmas fairy

star fairy

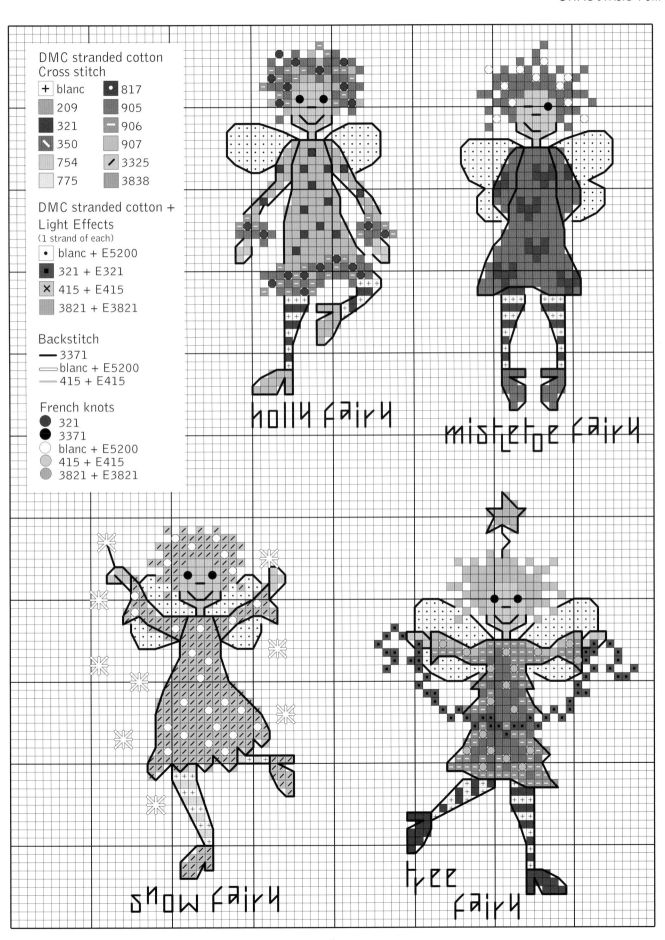

DMC stranded cotton
Cross stitch

+ blanc   • 817
  209   905
  321   906
  350   907
  754   3325
  775   3838

DMC stranded cotton +
Light Effects
(1 strand of each)

• blanc + E5200
■ 321 + E321
✕ 415 + E415
  3821 + E3821

Backstitch

— 3371
— blanc + E5200
— 415 + E415

French knots

  321
  3371
  blanc + E5200
  415 + E415
  3821 + E3821

holly fairy

mistletoe fairy

snow fairy

tree fairy

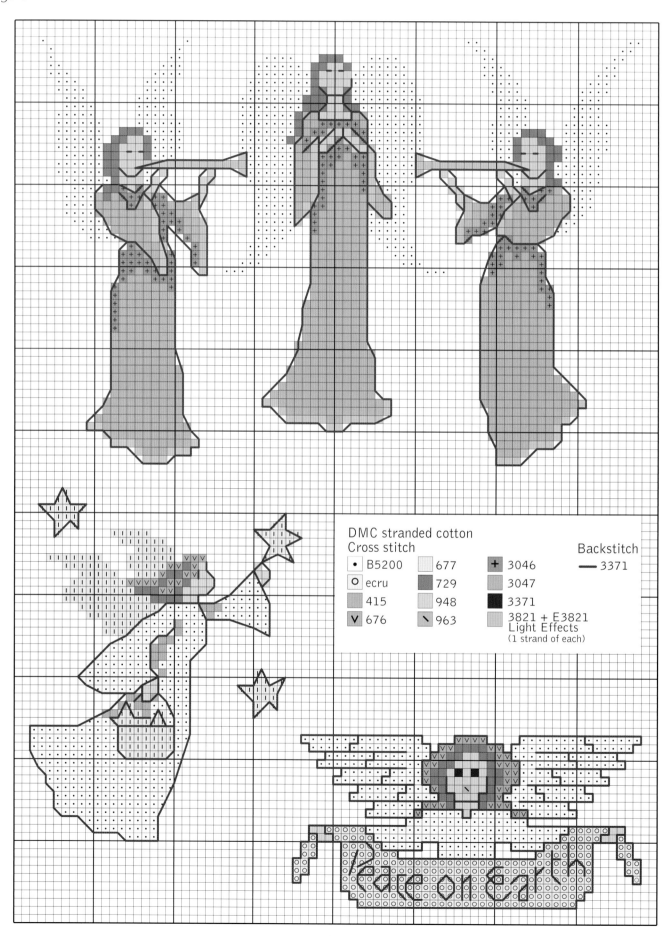

DMC stranded cotton
Cross stitch

Backstitch

- B5200
- ecru
- 415
- V 676

- 677
- 729
- 948
- \ 963

- + 3046
- 3047
- 3371
- 3821 + E3821
  Light Effects
  (1 strand of each)

— 3371

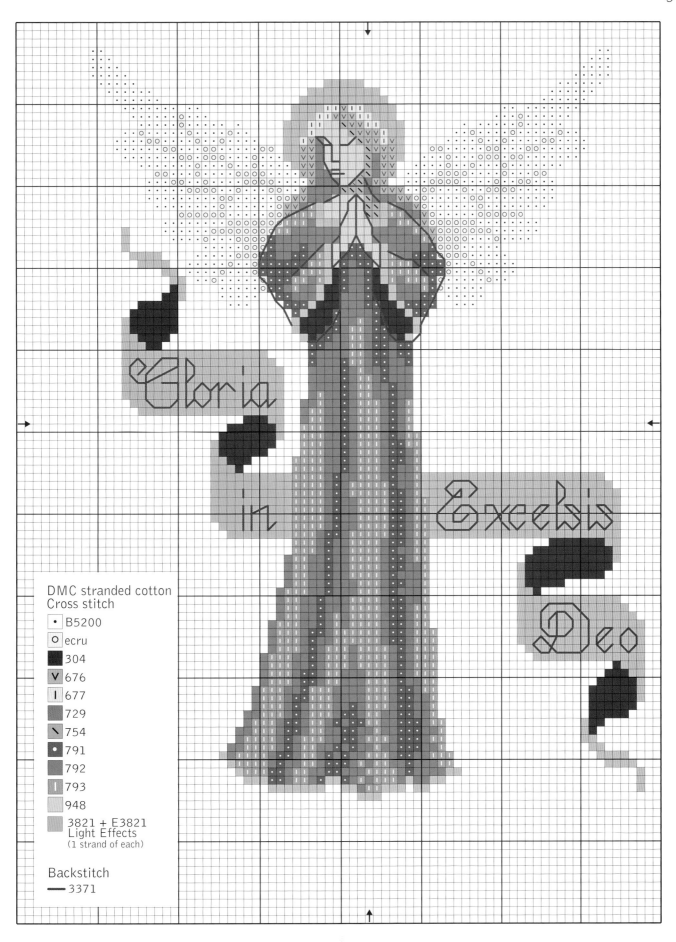

DMC stranded cotton
Cross stitch

- • B5200
- ○ ecru
- ■ 304
- V 676
- I 677
- 729
- ＼ 754
- 791
- 792
- I 793
- 948
- 3821 + E3821
  Light Effects
  (1 strand of each)

Backstitch
— 3371

Gloria in Excelsis Deo

sent via

Bear-Mail

It's Perfect!

Reindeer Spotting

Counting Snowflakes

DMC stranded cotton
Cross stitch

•	blanc		666	•	791	+	3862
◣	304		700		815		3863
	310	V	702		818	I	3864
O	334		704		962		
—	434	—	738		3325		
	436	U	775	O	3716		

DMC stranded cotton + Light Effects (1 strand of each)

/ blanc + E5200
✕ 3852 + E3852

French knots

● 3371

Backstitch
— 3371
= blanc + E5200
— 415 + E415

Too much stuffing!

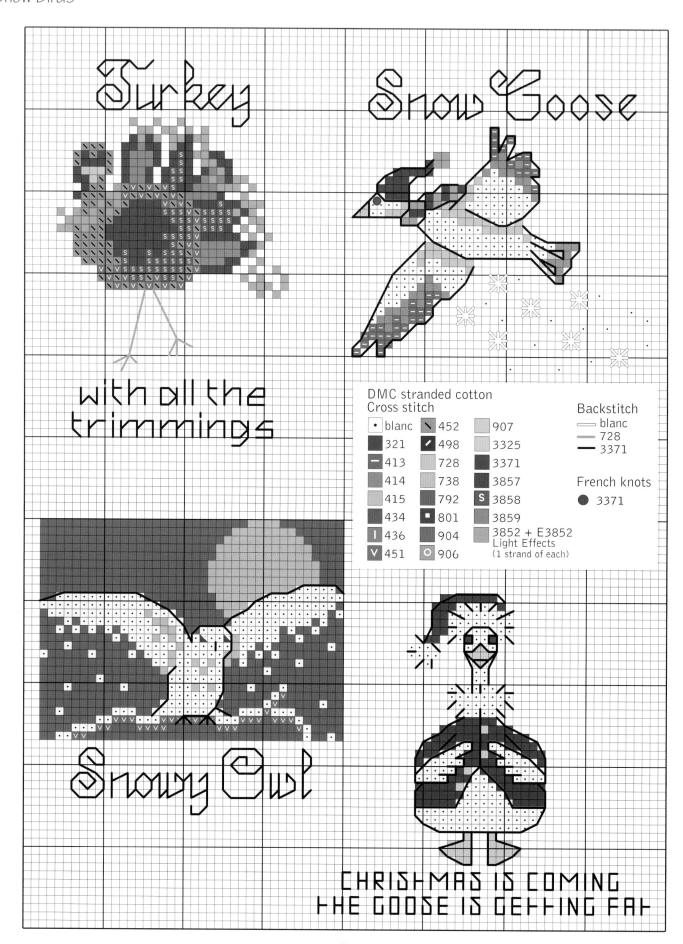

Turkey

Snow Goose

with all the
trimmings

Snowy Owl

CHRISTMAS IS COMING
THE GOOSE IS GETTING FAT

DMC stranded cotton
Cross stitch

• blanc	╲ 452	907
■ 321	╱ 498	3325
▬ 413	728	3371
414	738	3857
415	792	S 3858
434	■ 801	3859
I 436	904	3852 + E3852
V 451	O 906	Light Effects (1 strand of each)

Backstitch
══ blanc
— 728
— 3371

French knots
● 3371

I don't do Winter

Snow Bears

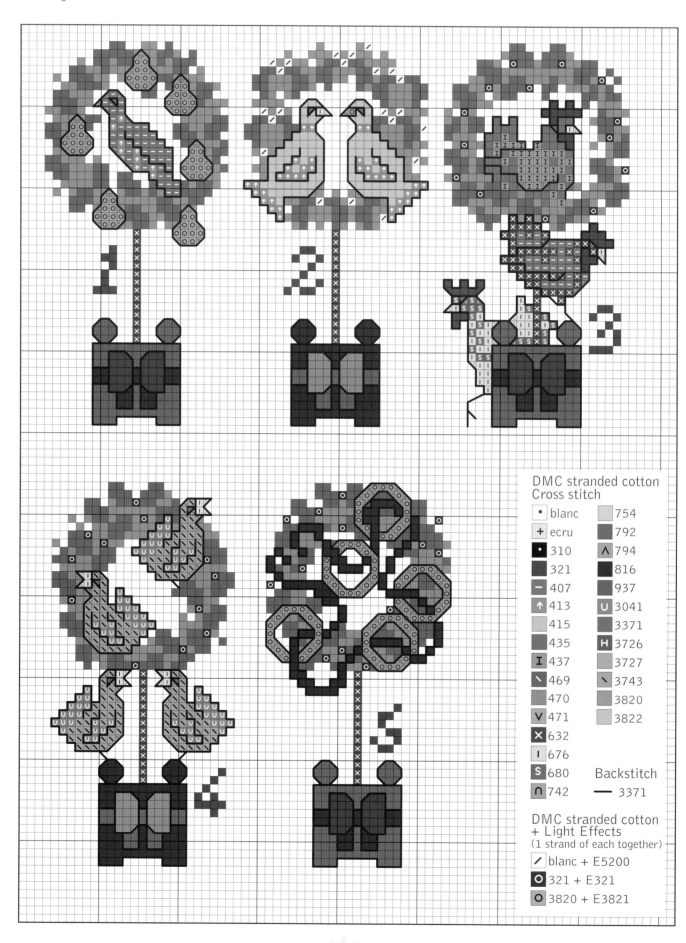

DMC stranded cotton
Cross stitch

•	blanc		754
+	ecru		792
●	310	∧	794
	321		816
—	407		937
↑	413	U	3041
	415		3371
	435	H	3726
I	437		3727
\	469	\	3743
	470		3820
V	471		3822
X	632		
I	676		
S	680		Backstitch
∩	742	—	3371

DMC stranded cotton
+ Light Effects
(1 strand of each together)

╱	blanc + E5200
⊙	321 + E321
○	3820 + E3821

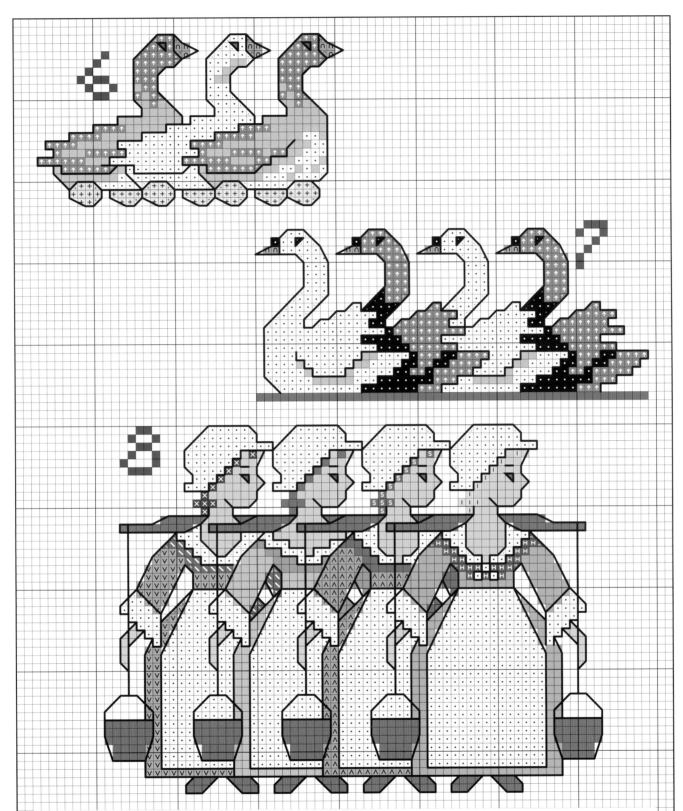

Geese, Swans and Milkmaids

These lines of figures are made up of a motif that is repeated with minor alterations. For example, the milkmaids are the same shape but have different necklines on their gowns. The geese and swans are worked in white and grey/black colourways.

To work the correct number of figures either work a mirror image of the line of motifs (omitting the last swan to get an odd number) or work the last motif the correct number of times, altering the colours.

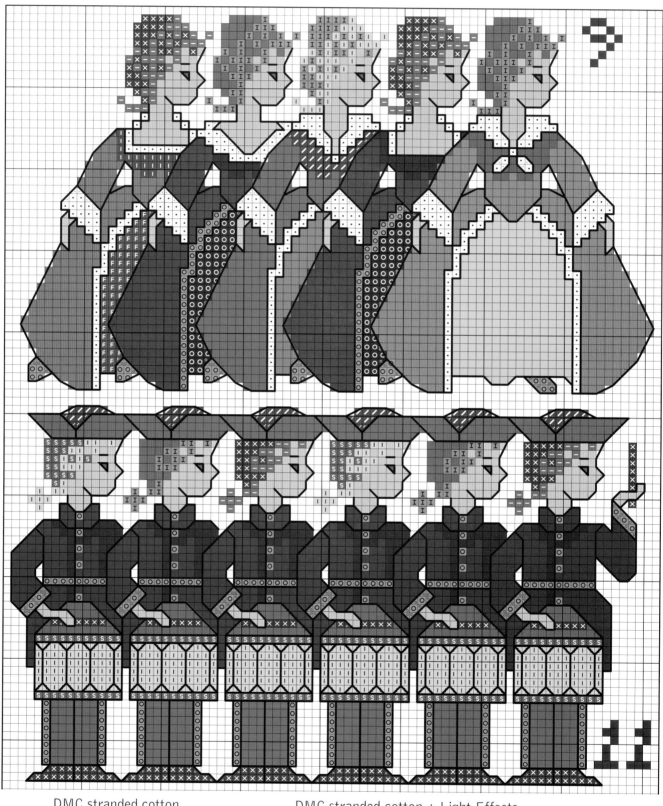

DMC stranded cotton
Cross stitch

• blanc	470	754	3371
321	V 471	∕ 791	3727
− 407	✗ 632	792	I 3834
435	I 676	816	3835
I 437	S 680	937	

DMC stranded cotton + Light Effects
(1 strand of each together)

∕ blanc + E5200	791 + E825
O 321 + E321	O 3820 + E3821
937 + E703	F 3834 + E3837

Backstitch

— 3371

Ladies, Lords, Drummers and Pipers

These lines of figures are made up of a motif that is repeated with minor alterations. For example, the ladies are the same shape but have different necklines. The lords have different necklines and sashes.

To work the correct number of figures either work a mirror image of the line of motifs (omitting the last figure to get an odd number of ladies and pipers) or work the last motif (the last two motifs of the lords) the correct number of times, altering colours and details.

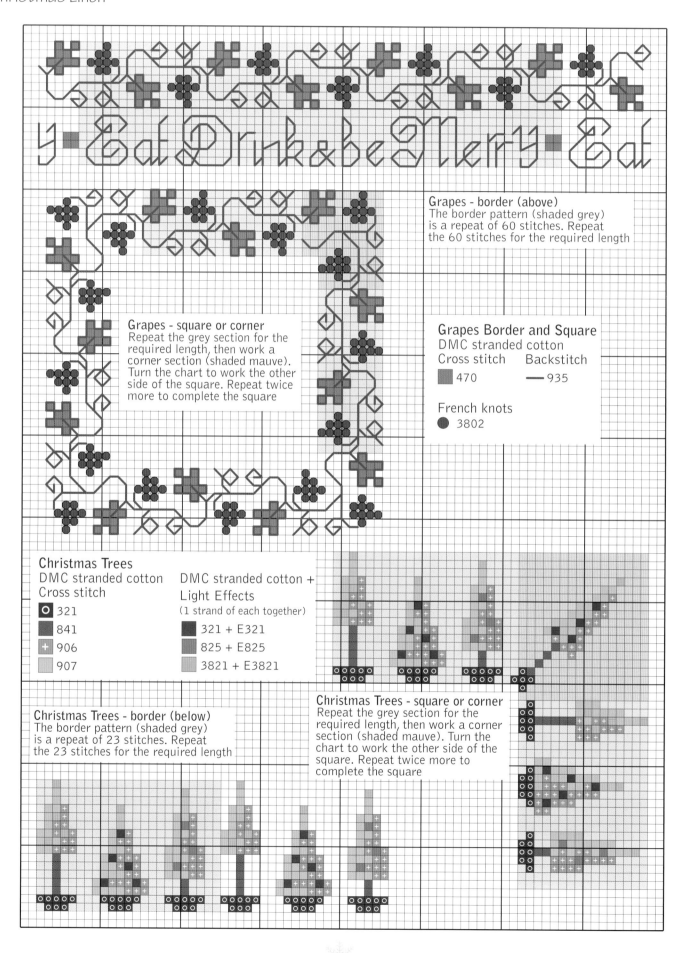

Grapes - border (above)
The border pattern (shaded grey)
is a repeat of 60 stitches. Repeat
the 60 stitches for the required length

Grapes - square or corner
Repeat the grey section for the
required length, then work a
corner section (shaded mauve).
Turn the chart to work the other
side of the square. Repeat twice
more to complete the square

Grapes Border and Square
DMC stranded cotton
Cross stitch   Backstitch
█ 470   — 935

French knots
● 3802

Christmas Trees
DMC stranded cotton   DMC stranded cotton +
Cross stitch   Light Effects
                             (1 strand of each together)
◉ 321   █ 321 + E321
█ 841   █ 825 + E825
+ 906   █ 3821 + E3821
█ 907

Christmas Trees - border (below)
The border pattern (shaded grey)
is a repeat of 23 stitches. Repeat
the 23 stitches for the required length

Christmas Trees - square or corner
Repeat the grey section for the
required length, then work a corner
section (shaded mauve). Turn the
chart to work the other side of the
square. Repeat twice more to
complete the square

Holly Border and Square
DMC stranded cotton
Cross stitch

- ◼ 321
- ◼ 791
- ◼ 3346

Mirror image
of holly motif

Holly - border (above)
The border pattern (shaded grey)
is a repeat of 26 stitches. Repeat
the 26 stitches for the required length

Holly - square or corner
Repeat the grey section for the
required length, then work a
corner section (shaded mauve).
Turn the chart to work the other
side of the square. Repeat twice
more to complete the square

WELCOME

Happy Holidays

MERRY EVERYTHING!

wishing you many

Mistletoe Moments

Meet me under the Mistletoe Hxx

DMC stranded cotton
Cross stitch

					Backstitch
•	blanc		666		3347	3347
	304		677		3829	3371
•	321		754	⊙	3863	
/	422		792			French knots
	434		904			● 3371

Alter the initial using
the alphabet on page 99

Friends and Family
are the best Gifts

*Jingle *All The *Way*

GrandKids
Spoiled
Here

HO HO HO
HO

Bah Humbug!

I don't do JOLLY!

DO NOT OPEN UNTIL CHRISTMAS

Christmas is Crackers!

DMC stranded cotton

Cross stitch
- 304
- 792
- 904
- 3347
- 3821 + E3821 Light Effects (1 strand of each)

Backstitch
- —— 3347
- —— 3371

French knots
- 3821 + E3821

JOY TO THE WORLD

WISE MEN still seek HIM

DMC stranded cotton

Cross stitch
- 905
- 498
- 3345
- 3371
- 3802
- 3852 + E3852 Light Effects (1 strand each)

Backstitch
- 3371
- 3852 + E3852 Light Effects (1 strand each)

AND THE ANGEL SAID UNTO THEM,
FEAR NOT:FOR,BEHOLD,I BRING YOU
GOOD TIDINGS OF GREAT JOY,
WHICH SHALL BE TO ALL PEOPLE
FOR UNTO YOU IS BORN THIS DAY
IN THE CITY OF DAVID A SAVIOUR,
WHICH IS CHRIST THE LORD
LUKE2:10-11

And on this day
a Child was born

PEACE

Peace on Earth
Goodwill
to all Men

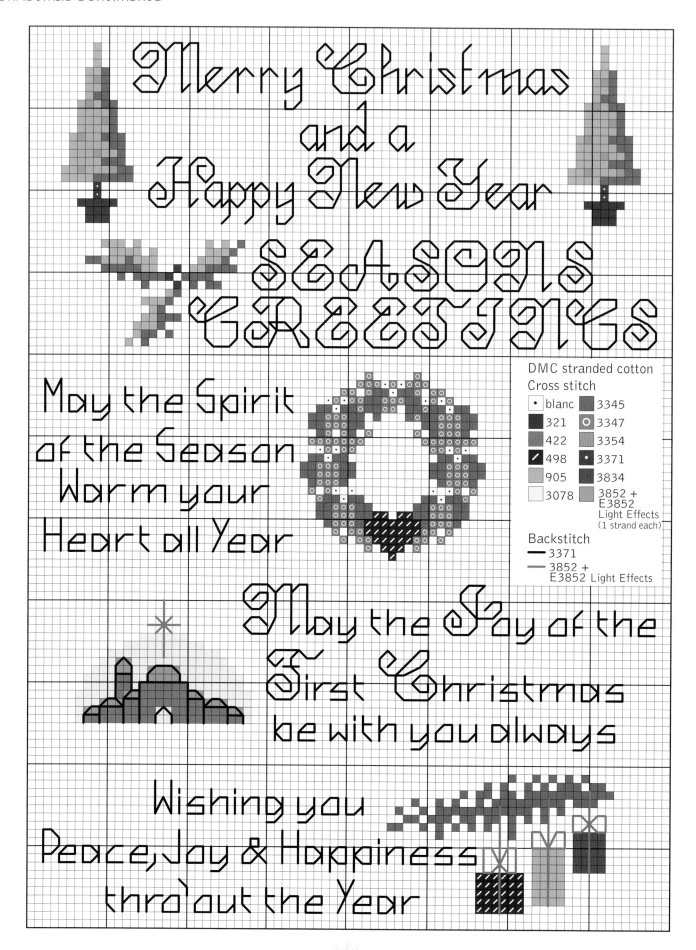

'tis the
season
to be jolly

Trumpets Sound
& Angels Sing
LISTEN TO WHAT THEY SAY
AND MAN WILL LIVE FOR EVERMORE BECAUSE OF
Christmas Day

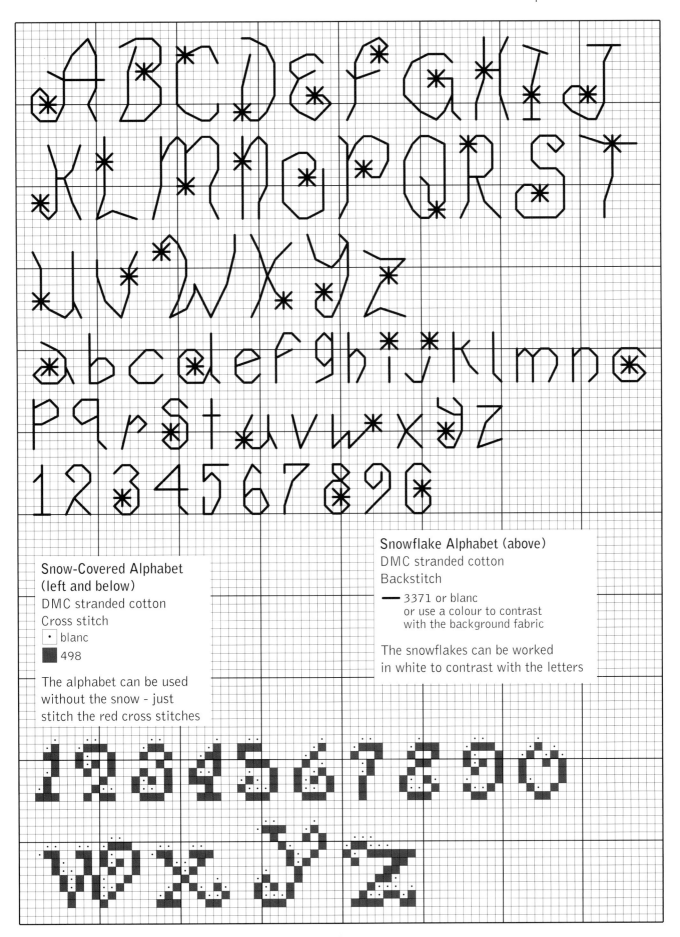

**Snow-Covered Alphabet
(left and below)**
DMC stranded cotton
Cross stitch
- · blanc
- ■ 498

The alphabet can be used
without the snow - just
stitch the red cross stitches

Snowflake Alphabet (above)
DMC stranded cotton
Backstitch

— 3371 or blanc
   or use a colour to contrast
   with the background fabric

The snowflakes can be worked
in white to contrast with the letters

Change the colour of the alphabet to suit your project

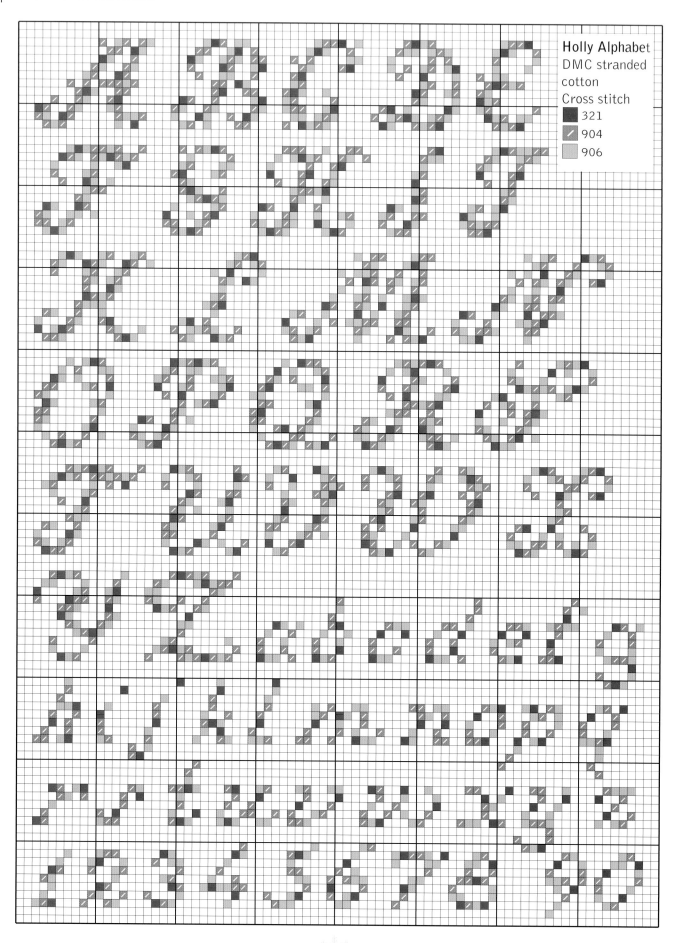

Holly Alphabet
DMC stranded cotton
Cross stitch

■ 321
╱ 904
▨ 906

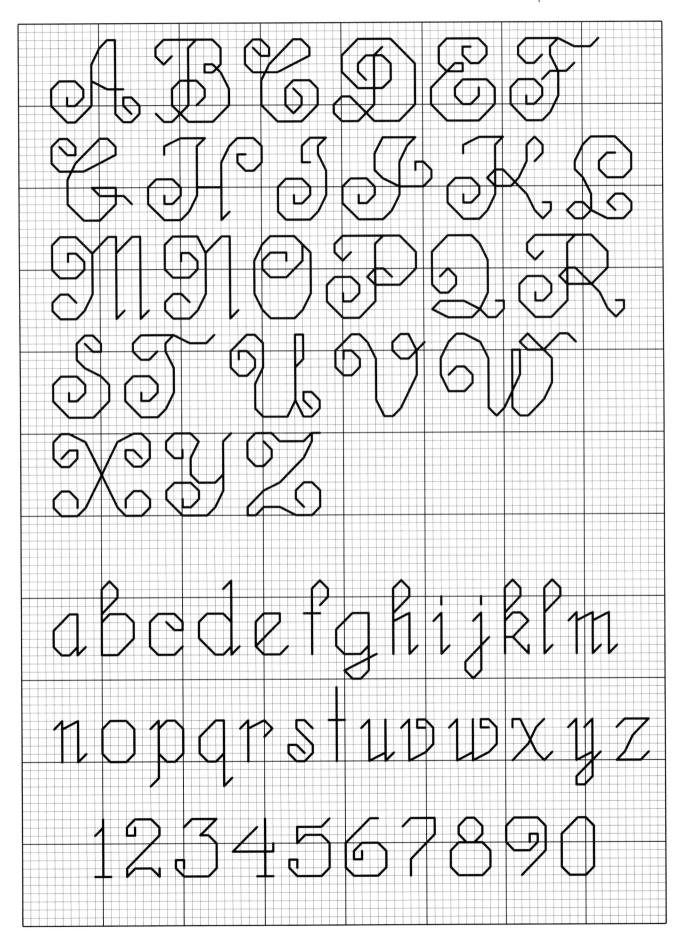

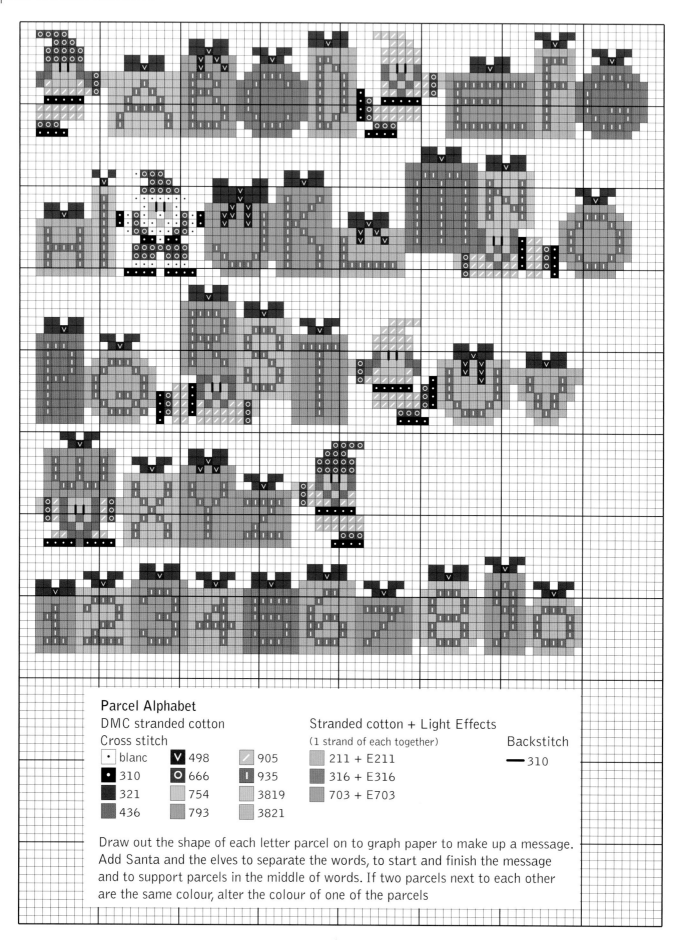

Parcel Alphabet

DMC stranded cotton
Cross stitch

· blanc	**V** 498	/ 905	
■ 310	**O** 666	I 935	
■ 321	754	3819	
436	793	3821	

Stranded cotton + Light Effects
(1 strand of each together)

211 + E211
316 + E316
703 + E703

Backstitch
— 310

Draw out the shape of each letter parcel on to graph paper to make up a message.
Add Santa and the elves to separate the words, to start and finish the message
and to support parcels in the middle of words. If two parcels next to each other
are the same colour, alter the colour of one of the parcels

Snow Alphabet (above)
DMC stranded cotton
Cross stitch   Backstitch

• blanc   —— 318

▨ 800

Use the letters as ice blocks to build a message.
Place the letters next to each other and words on top
of each other. Use the grey backstitch to outline the
shapes created, rather than outlining individual letters.
See page 40 for an example

Medieval Alphabet
DMC stranded cotton
Cross stitch

▨ 3345

Backstitch
—— 3852 + E3852
(1 strand of each)

Suppliers

The following suppliers will have the materials and equipment you need to work the designs in this book. Contact the manufacturers for your local stockist or find local stockists and mail order information on their websites.

UK

DMC Creative World Ltd
Pullman Road, Wigston, Leicester, LE18 2DY
Tel: 0116 2811040
www.dmc.com
For DMC fabrics, bands, threads and ready-made Aida items

Coats Crafts UK
PO Box 22, Lingfield Estate, McMullen Road, Darlington,
County Durham DL1 1YQ
Tel: 01325 365457 (for stockists)
For Anchor threads

Madeira threads (UK) Ltd
PO Box 6, Thirsk, North Yorkshire YO7 3YX
Tel: 01845 524880
www.madeira.co.uk
For Madeira threads

Willow Fabrics
95 Town Lane, Mobberley, Knutsford, Cheshire WA16 7HH
Tel: 0800 0567811
www.willowfabrics.com
For embroidery fabrics and threads

Framecraft Miniatures Ltd
Unit 3, Isis House, Lindon Road, Brownhills,
West Midlands, WS8 7BW
Tel: 01543 360842
www.framecraft.com
For ready-made items and Mill Hill beads

Impress Cards & Craft Materials
Slough Farm, Westhall, Suffolk, IP19 8RN
Tel: 01986 781422
Email: sales@impresscards.co.uk
www.impresscards.com
For card blanks

Craft Creations Ltd
Ingersoll House, Delamare Road, Cheshunt,
Hertfordshire, EN8 9HD
Tel: 01992 781900
Email: enquiries@craftcreations.com
www.craftcreations.com
For card blanks

Memory Keepsakes
Shakeford Mill, Hinstock, Market Drayton, Shropshire TF9 2SP
Tel: 01630 638342
www.memorykeepsakes.co.uk
For card-making supplies

USA

The DMC Corporation
10 Port Kearney, South Kearney, NJ 070732
Tel: 973-589 0606
www.dmc-usa.com
For DMC threads and fabrics

Mill Hill, a division of Wichelt Imports Inc.
N162 Hwy 35, Stoddard WI 54658
Tel: 608 788 4600
www.millhill.com
For Mill Hill beads and ready-made items

Acknowledgments

I would like to thank DMC Creative World Ltd, UK, for their generosity in supplying all fabrics and threads used for the projects in this book.

About the Author

Claire studied knitwear design at college before joining the design team at DMC, and finally going freelance. Claire's work has appeared in several magazines, including *Cross Stitch Magic*. Her designs also feature in six David & Charles books: *Cross Stitch Greetings Cards, Cross Stitch Alphabets, Cross Stitch Angels, Cross Stitch Fairies, Magical Cross Stitch* and *Quick to Stitch Cross Stitch Cards,* and in her books *Cross Stitch Card Collection* and *Picture Your Pet in Cross Stitch*, also published by David & Charles. Claire lives in Gunnislake, Cornwall. Contact Claire at www.clairecrompton.co.uk

Index